President's Circle 2005-2006

Thank you for your generous gift
to Wellesley College.

Wellesley College offers a unique and challenging
education to women of talent and commitment.
Your sustaining support enables Wellesley students
to experience the rewards of intellectual engagement
and personal growth that will not only transform
their lives but will also inspire their contributions
to communities around the world.

Diana Chapman Walsh

Diana Chapman Walsh '66
President

Nehoiden Golf Club

and the History of Golf at Wellesley College

1893–2005

Nehoiden Golf Club

and the History of Golf at Wellesley College

1893–2005

The Nehoiden Centennial

History Committee

Editor

Martin A. Padley

Executive Committee

Scott Birney

Martin A. Padley

Hal Phillips

Shirley Quinn

Advisory Committee

James Donahue

Doris Gardner

James Olson

Hal Phillips, III

Eric Sinisalo

Mert Young

A fall view across Nehoiden's 8th, 7th, and 6th holes toward Galen Stone Tower on the College campus

This book was researched, written, and produced by the Nehoiden Centennial History Committee, a volunteer group comprised of members of Nehoiden Golf Club and is not the sole product of Wellesley College.

Published by Wellesley College, Wellesley, Massachusetts 02481-8203
Copies of this publication may be purchased by writing to the publisher.

ISBN 0-9744898-2-4

Library of Congress Control Number: 2005924515

Printed in Hong Kong

To Diana Chapman Walsh

We dedicate this history to Diana Chapman Walsh, whose fondness for golf and Nehoiden reflect our own attachment to the game and the place. During her presidency, Nehoiden has undergone steady improvement, and she is familiar with the course from a golfer's perspective as was President Caroline Hazard more than 100 years ago when it was first built.

In 1900, to express their gratitude for President Hazard's support, the members of the Wellesley Golf Club made her an honorary member of their links. We would happily extend the same consideration to Diana Chapman Walsh were she not already a member in good standing. In place of an honorary membership, we are pleased to dedicate this history to her.

Diana Chapman Walsh

For the golfers of Nehoiden—past, present, and future

Contents

ABOVE: *A fall view of the 2nd fairway from the old wooden bridge on the 3rd hole. In 2005, this bridge was replaced by a wider and stronger structure that serves both the 2nd and 3rd holes.*

Acknowledgments

This history would have been impossible without the help of many people, most of whom are connected in one way or another with Nehoiden.

Because the Nehoiden Centennial History Committee felt that including many photographs was important, this book is as much a pictorial as a history. A special note of thanks is due to all who graciously agreed to have their photographs taken and especially to those whose photos do not appear in these pages. We were not always certain of our direction and ended up taking many more photos than we possibly could have used.

Our first and most formal note of thanks must go to Wellesley College Archivist Wilma Slaight. Her knowledge of the College's wonderful archives and clear understanding of our mission were invaluable in our quest for photographs and source materials from the early years. Her persistence and dedication to our cause have unquestionably resulted in some wonderful finds. Our thanks and appreciation must also go to Assistant Archivist Jean Berry for her support and willingness to pitch in whenever Wilma wasn't available.

Several alumnae gave us some unexpected assistance, notably Melinda M. Ponder '66, the biographer of Katharine Lee Bates '80, whom we met by chance in the archives, and College Trustee Amalie Moses Kass '49, who pointed us in the direction of *our* Dr. Channing as the result of a chance phone call.

We were also aided by the College's Department of Physical Education, Recreation and Athletics; its director Louise O'Neal; golf team coach and instructor Bill McInerney; Professor of Physical Education Ann Batchelder, and golf team captain Victoria Lyo '05.

The recollections of many golfers and nongolfers have been very useful to us including those of Fred Nolan, who played here in the 1940s, and Ward Fearnside, our resident ball hawk, who has known the course intimately since 1919. Nehoiden members and friends were also helpful with ideas, verifying facts, and observations about the club, the course, and the members.

Of considerable assistance were the historical societies of Dedham, Needham, and Natick, and especially the Wellesley Historical Society and its well-informed director, Laurel Nilsen Sparks. The resourceful reference librarians at the Wellesley Public Library also provided a good deal of skilled, useful, and cheerful help.

A special note of thanks must go to Elizabeth Hunnewell, former President of the Wellesley Historical Society, the Hunnewell family, and to historian Allyson Hayward, who has done extensive research on the Hunnewells and their estates and who found the photo of Florence Boit.

We are particularly grateful for the approval and good wishes of Nehoiden's Joint Committee, whose former chair, Will Reed, supported our efforts from mid-2001 until after he retired in 2002. The current chair, Patricia Byrne, enthusiastically continued Reed's support through the final approval process, and Romi Cumming, publications director, oversaw a thorough copy editing. Support also came from many others at the College including Sheilah Ciraso in maintenance services, Traci Robie in physical plant, Mary Ann Hill in public information, and Alice Hummer of the alumnae magazine.

Professor of Art History and Nehoiden member and neighbor Peter Fergusson reviewed our drafts on the history and grounds, Allyson Hayward reviewed the sections on the Hunnewells, Laurel Sparks the portions that include town history, and former Nehoiden Manager Tony Oteri the history and course description. Nehoiden members Adele Beggs, Phil and Nancye Connor, Marilyn Nutting, and Tom Kelley helped with proofing—it was Tom who first suggested that Nehoiden's founding could be considered earlier than 1900.

Massachusetts golf historians Dick Haskell and John English, a former president of the Massachusetts Golf Association (MGA), were very helpful with area golf history. Louis Newell, librarian and archivist at The Country Club, and David Normoyle of the United States Golf Association (USGA) history department also made helpful contributions to our cause. Both Normoyle and Haskell agree that the founding of Nehoiden Golf Club can be traced to 1893.

While their names probably should have appeared at the top of our list, we reserve a special note of appreciation for Patrick Willoughby, Nehoiden Manager and Associate Director of Physical Plant, and to the entire Nehoiden grounds crew and staff for their insights, recollections, assistance, and good cheer.

Our committee includes several people who should be singled out for their contributions. Member Hal Phillips conceived the idea for the book in 2001 and presented it to a number of Nehoiden enthusiasts who found his concept appealing, including retired Wellesley College Professor of Astronomy Emeritus Scott Birney, former

Class Dean Shirley Quinn, and Wellesley Vice President of Finance Will Reed. Hal took many photos and interviewed a great many people. Hal's son, known as Little Hal, lent his writing ability to our first drafts and reviewed Scott Birney's research notes and early findings. Shirley Quinn pitched in with research and used her editing skills to review three years' worth of revisions to the text. Former Men's Group President Jim Donahue, along with Eric Sinisalo, Jim Olson, Shirley Quinn, and Scott Birney, helped with information about the course and the College. Retired printing sales rep Mert Young gave helpful advice; Nehoiden spirit Doris Gardner shared her reminiscences; and Nehoiden regular, Martin Padley, provided his design, production, photography, research, and writing skills to get the book into final shape and ready for publication. A special note of appreciation is owed to Stephanie Bradley, the graphic designer who conceived and executed the design, and to Terry Cracknell AIA, an architect and architectural illustrator, who drew our illustrated maps and plans.

For whatever errors exist—historical, factual, and grammatical—the committee accepts full responsibility and is grateful for any and all mulligans.

It is also fitting that we express a note of appreciation to Pauline and Henry Fowle Durant, whose vision for Wellesley College included emphasis on health and exercise, as well as to William Nehoiden and the Massachusett tribe, the original stewards of this land.

Finally, we take our hats off to Lucile Eaton Hill and Edith Gordon Walker '00 for their dedication and inspired activism. Where would we be without them?

ABOVE: *The Nehoiden Centennial History Committee often met in the front parlor of Hal and Lucy Phillips' home on Dover Road, with its views of the course and 1890s ambiance. Counter-clockwise from the bottom step are Shirley Quinn, Doris Gardner, Scott Birney, Hal Phillips, Martin Padley, Jim Olson, Eric Sinisalo, Jim Donahue, and Mert Young (not shown, Hal Phillips III).*

Introduction

The Nehoiden Centennial History Committee began this book in 2001 to commemorate the club's 100th year in 2003. When we began our research, we had no idea that we would ultimately learn that the course we play opened in the fall of 1900 and that it was the direct successor to a course that had been laid out on the College campus in 1894 for the use of a club that was formed in 1893. Golf historians agree that Nehoiden Golf Club's founding can be traced to 1893.

Nehoiden has always been a modest golf club. Indeed, there is little outward evidence to suggest that it can be traced to 1893 and the dawn of golf in Massachusetts or that the land it sits on was close to some of the earliest events in colonial history.

Take the 6th green, for example. It is near the spot on Waban Brook where John Eliot, "the Apostle to the Indians," built a sawmill in 1651, and it is directly across the street from Homestead, the summer home of the College's founders, Pauline and Henry Fowle Durant, in the 1850s when they first lived in West Needham (as Wellesley was then called).

The Durants were wealthy and cultivated people, but when their young son died in 1864, they underwent a dramatic life change and decided to devote their considerable wealth and extensive Wellesley estate to a women's college. The Durants were very aware that women at that time were often poorly educated. Today,

Wellesley's stated mission "to provide an excellent liberal arts education for women who will make a difference in the world" reflects the Durants' original purpose. One of their firm beliefs was that the students should get plenty of exercise to meet the challenges of a rigorous education to maintain their equanimity and become physically equal to the task.

The College's first golf course was laid out in 1894 by Dr. Walter Channing, a noted Boston psychiatrist, and a Mr. Hunnewell, most likely Arthur, who had built the first course in Massachusetts and is discussed in Chapter One. Dr. Channing is worthy of a closer look, for while he does not appear in the annals of golf (as Arthur Hunnewell does), he is important in the world of mental health. A prominent Boston psychiatrist, he founded a number of mental hospitals and sanitariums in the Boston area (including one in Wellesley), initiated legislation for the treatment of the mentally ill, was the founder of the Boston Society of Psychiatry and Neurology, and was a proponent of exercise in the public schools. He was a firm believer in physical exercise as a means of promoting mental health—as were the Durants.

Dr. Channing is interesting partly because he is typical of the people the Durants surrounded themselves with when they singlehandedly took on the immense task of creating a college at their own expense.

Nehoiden's centennial? You decide.

Nehoiden is surely a tribute to 19th century drive, wealth, and enlightenment, but it is also a place with a rich and unexpected history. It was first a campground for Native Americans; then a farm from earliest colonial times until well into the 19th century; and finally part and parcel of a vibrant college that would grow to have a strong national reputation.

When this project began, in the fall of 2001, it was clear that the Wellesley College archives would be of importance, and many hours were spent there going over old memos, minutes, plans, scrapbooks, yearbooks, newspaper clippings, and the like. At times the information we sought was frustratingly nonexistent. Yet a surprising amount of material was sitting there, just waiting to be found.

When golf architect Wayne Stiles' plans for Nehoiden were examined, they became an important tool not only because they showed how Nehoiden might have been, but also because they showed what the course was like in 1927. Over the years, changes have been made to the 1900 layout: three holes were totally redone, Fuller Brook was straightened, and in 1964 the entire course was renumbered. There are members who play today who remember the old numbering system and their recollections—and the recollections of many others—have been an invaluable part of our research.

Because Nehoiden's history is tied up with the history of the College, the town, and our neighbors the Hunnewells, our research went further afield than we first would have thought possible. Some questions we found answers to; others remain mysteries.

All sorts of people stroll through our pages, and many have walked across our fairways, including John Eliot, William Nehoiden, Waban, the Dewings, the Hunnewells, the Durants, Dr. Channing, the Olmsteds, Katharine Lee Bates, John Updike, and many others from all walks of life.

What emerges is the story of a sometimes quirky golf course with a fascinating past. When all is said and done, Nehoiden Golf Club is very much in a class of its own: unpretentious yet with a startlingly rich heritage.

Those who play Nehoiden would agree that it is unlike most other golf courses—from an absence of starting times to an excess of out-of-bounds rules. The club's centennial year is just as curious, and it is very likely that 2003 was not Nehoiden's 100th after all. Here are some facts that the Centennial History Committee has unearthed to help you decide:

1893 A golf club is formed at Wellesley College but does not appear to have a formal place to play.

1894 What could best be described as a practice facility for golf is built near Lake Waban, probably in the spring. In August, a golf course is laid out on the campus—it starts out near Shakespeare House, goes past the chapel, up to the observatory, then runs along Central Street.

1900 A new course is built across Washington Street with funds raised by members of the Wellesley Golf Club. The new golf course opens for play in October 1900, an event commemorated in several newspapers (see extract below and, for a full transcript, the Appendix).

1903 The Wellesley Golf Club is reorganized with new officers, and its affairs are now overseen by the College's Joint Committee.

1908 The Wellesley Golf Club falls on hard times in 1906, ceases to exist for a year, and is reorganized in its current form in 1908. During 1907, golf continues on the course as a College sport.

1927 The Wellesley Golf Club is renamed Nehoiden.

A unique feature of this Wellesley Golf Club is the combining in one large elastic association of 'town and gown.' The common meeting ground of a golf course opens a happy prospect of enlarged opportunity for closer assimilation between two bodies, naturally separated, in the main, by differences of pursuit.

The Boston Evening Transcript
July 25, 1900

The History of Nehoiden

Golf arrived at Wellesley College in the fall of 1893 thanks to an overcrowded gymnasium and an imaginative director of physical training. It is very likely that Wellesley had the first college golf club in the country, and it was saved from extinction in 1900 by the inspired leadership of a College senior with a flare for the dramatic.

Before the spring of 1893, Wellesley athletics were in the doldrums. The gymnasium was overcrowded, and sports were limited to rowing and tennis. The *Wellesley Magazine*, a student literary publication, editorialized in June 1893 that the key to getting more students to exercise was to make exercise more interesting and enjoyable, and it asked its readers, "Who will find the key?"

The person holding the key was Lucile Eaton Hill, Wellesley's first Director of Physical Training. Described as a dynamic woman with a good sense of humor and a magnetic personality, she was trying to cope with an impossibly crowded gymnasium where, for three hours a week, exercises were a requirement for the 700-plus students at the College. She concluded that if she couldn't fit enough students into the gym, then perhaps she could take them outdoors. In the spring of 1893 she had formed a bicycle club, and when she returned to the campus in the fall of 1893, she introduced golf and basketball clubs, to the delight of the students. There is no record of where golf was played or who taught it, but there was plenty of open space to hit balls and Hill believed in the value of expert instruction even for crew, an established sport.

That November the *Wellesley Magazine* reported that "the tireless and zealous spirit who has established golf and basket-ball [*sic*] on our campus has not been daunted by the cramped quarters of the gymnasium, but has seized on the wider opportunities of a width of ground."

But it was difficult to play basketball on uneven ground. Hill's solution was to build a level, multi-purpose playing field—an "outdoor gymnasium"—for basketball, golf, running, and bicycling. To be called the Playstead, it would be located on a three-acre site between Lake Waban and Music Hall (now the Schneider Student Center). The freshmen class was very enthusiastic about the Playstead and raised the $1,500 required to build it; Hill posted security for the project with her own funds. The Playstead opened in 1894 and was encircled by an eight-lane running and bicycle track which could have also been used for "scientific pedestrianism"—a term that may have been used in jest, but pinpoints Hill's approach to sports.

AT LEFT: *Lucile Eaton Hill came to the College in 1882 and remained until 1909. As the Director of Physical Training she initiated many of Wellesley's sports programs and remained steadfast to her credo that exercise is the source of good health.*

FACING PAGE: *This photo of "The golf team of Wellesley College" appeared in the* New York Herald *in 1897. In the center, wearing a charming hat, a starburst brooch, and a confident expression, is Edith Gordon Walker '00, President of the Wellesley Golf Club from 1898 to 1900.*

Hill soon introduced even more sports to lure reluctant students from their sedentary ways. There were clubs for fencing, archery, baseball, bowling, and natural dancing (something which would become a part of Wellesley's annual Tree Day pageant for years to come), but the most popular were crew, basketball, and golf. All of this new activity was in line with the mission of both the College and Hill: to improve strength and health.

Hill had triumphed over the crowded gymnasium, and she greatly expanded student interest in sports.

Later, the usually buoyant Hill became disenchanted with basketball (it was too vigorous and competitive) *and* with golf (it was "the aristocrat" of sport: there were too few courses and most were for the well-to-do). But sometimes, things develop a momentum their own.

A small item in *The Boston Evening Transcript* announced some big news on August 30, 1894: a golf course was being laid out at the College. The item reads in its entirety: "Golf has reached Wellesley. Last year a gentleman much interested in athletics sent a man there to teach the young women golf and the interest shown was so great that this year he has generously given a full golf outfit to the college and the links are now being laid out."

More than five years later, the Boston *Sunday Herald* of May 20, 1900, ran a feature on the course reporting that it was "laid out through the kindness of Dr. Walter Channing of Brookline and Mr. Hunnewell of Wellesley." While it does not say which Mr. Hunnewell, it was probably Arthur (see page 8), who had laid out several links

including The Country Club's first course in 1893. Dr. Channing, a member of The Country Club with several Hunnewells, was a prominent psychiatrist who believed in a close connection between exercise and mental health. Perhaps the donor was Dr. Channing: he had already given two clay tennis courts to the College and he sat on the visiting committee of the department of physical training with two other physicians and a former governor of the state. But the donor could have been Mr. Hunnewell.

Meanwhile, golf had become all the rage. The *New York Herald* of June 13, 1897, wrote that "Golf Will Be the Prevailing Sport This Year at Wellesley College" and "For certain temperaments and for certain kinds of weariness it has been found that a quiet game is the best sort of a tonic." The *Sunday Herald* quoted from the 1900 College yearbook: "On any fine and sunny afternoon, the observer may see short-skirted* maidens brandishing sticks with a menacing air or wildly rooting up turf in their enthusiasm, while others go poking furtively among the woods and boggy places, seeking for 'that old ball I lost.'"

The *Sunday Herald* gave a description of the links and announced, if belatedly, "The Wellesley Golf Club Has a Very Picturesque Course" noting that the grounds, "with their broad level stretches of campus, skirted by woodlands, smooth meadows, crossed by tiny brooks, and rolling upland fields, present unusual opportunities for the popular game and have the added charm of beauty of surroundings." (See Appendix for transcript.)

Unhappily, the days of this reportedly idyllic course were numbered. The College was expanding. When the chapel, observatory, and several other buildings were being built between 1897 and 1900, they eliminated or cut into the holes on the campus course. The members became increasingly dismayed, as did golfers from the town and the Dana Hall School who played as guests.

Would the "short-skirted maidens" of the Wellesley Golf Club shed a tear and watch helplessly as their course got whittled away to nothing? No, they would not! Quite the contrary. They decided to take action, raise money, and build a new golf course.

But first, they would put on a play.

AT TOP: *This view from the grounds of Mrs. Durant's house was taken in the late 1880s. The Playstead was built on a three-acre site near Music Hall (left of center) and close to Lake Waban. Alumnae were upset that the Playstead had been built over a buttercup meadow and protested that it marred the beauty of the campus. At best the field could have been used for practice, putting, and probably for hitting balls into Lake Waban. College Hall is to the left and Stone Hall is at right.*

ABOVE LEFT: *Launcelot Cressy Servos, "the well-known golf professional," gave lessons at the College in 1899 and 1900. He not only wrote a book on how to play golf and laid out a golf course in Clearwater, Florida, but he also wrote a play, a novel, and an opera.*

ABOVE RIGHT: *Anna Cross '00 and Ethell Lentell '00 are on a hillside of the campus course with a pile of golf clubs at their feet.*

* Skirt lengths for golf in 1900 are shown at left and on pages 4 and 5.

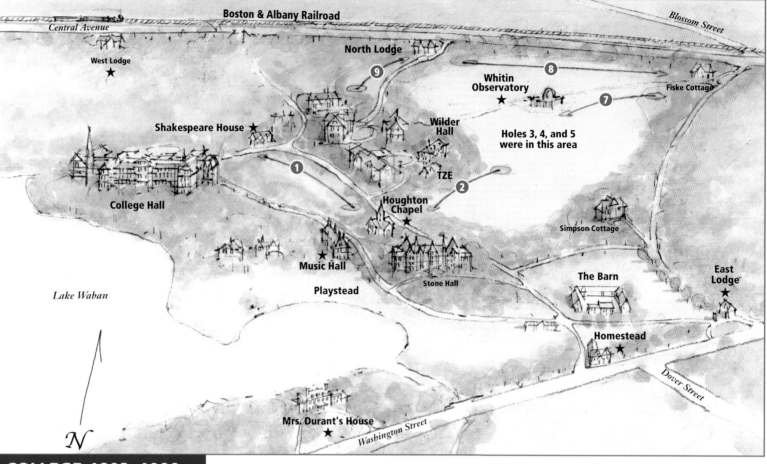

— MAP Notes —

The Golf Course
The hole locations shown here are based on an article in *The Sunday Herald* of June 13, 1900, which is the only description we have of the campus course. See Appendix.

Larger Type
Building names in larger type are referred to in the book.

The Barn
Originally on the Durant estate, it was later downsized and became Dower Hall, a dormitory.

North Lodge
It was used as a waiting room for the "electrics"—the trolley cars of the Natick and Cochituate Street Railway. See below, at right.

Tau Zeta Epsilon (TZE)
Was later moved elsewhere

★ = Still exists

GOLF AT WELLESLEY COLLEGE 1893–1900

In 1893 there was a golf club at the College, but it is not known where golf was played. Most likely in the spring of 1894, the Playstead, an "outdoor gymnasium," opened for golf and other sports.

On August 30, 1894, *The Boston Evening Transcript* reported that a campus golf course was being laid out, and *The Sunday Herald* of May 20, 1900, describes its holes—but makes no mention of the 6th, which was apparently no longer in existence when the article was written. The 6th hole appears to have been near Whitin Observatory and may have been eliminated when it was built (between 1899 and 1900). See Appendix.

The Boston Evening Transcript of July 25, 1900, reported that "the college grounds have been growing more and more inadequate as the course has several times been abridged, owing to the erection of new buildings, notably the Houghton Memorial Chapel and the Wilder [*sic*] observatory."

At Left: *The division between the fairway and rough is quite distinct on the 2nd hole of the campus golf course. Left of center, the building that can just barely be seen through the trees is the original Tau Zeta Epsilon Society house.*

Below: *The streetcars that ran along Central Avenue (as it was then called) would have been useful for the townspeople and the Dana Hall students who played golf as guests.*

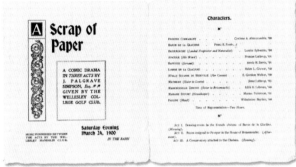

Edith Gordon Walker '00 (or E. Gordon Walker as she preferred to be known) was president of the Wellesley Golf Club from 1898 to 1900, and she was a force to be reckoned with. She organized the fund-raising play *and* had a starring role in it. An undated newspaper clipping of the time explained that "it was Miss Walker's duty, as club president, to give the introductory address and she had a leading role in the part of Mlle. Suzanne de Ruseville, which the Boston dailies in reporting, spoke of in pleasant, complimentary terms."

Walker was also president of the Mandolin Club, which serenaded the audience during the two intermissions, although it appears that she refrained from joining in and playing an instrument.

The Sunday Herald reported that "The club has given a brilliantly successful play, to raise money for improving the course, and the result is $150 toward the establishment of a new links, if it is finally deemed advisable."

The play was held in The Barn, a building on the campus that was used for dances and theatricals. More than 500 people attended, including over 100 from outside the College. The $150 that the club netted from ticket, candy, and souvenir sales should have been enough to construct their new course, considering that it cost $50 to build a six-hole experimental course at The Country Club in 1893.

In May, the newspaper reported that "a course of 3,000 yards could easily be laid out" just north of the campus. But there was nothing definite yet.

In June 1900, golf at Wellesley College began to change dramatically.

The club got permission to withdraw from the Wellesley Athletic Association which Lucile Eaton Hill had formed in 1896 to provide a broader structure for the clubs. Next, it successfully petitioned the trustees to build a nine-hole course across Washington Street on College-owned land. The club became an organization that was completely different from anything else on campus, with a membership that included students, faculty, town residents, and students at the Dana Hall School. The club president was a town resident, and the vice president was on the faculty. The plan was to keep an arm's-length relationship with the College, lease the land for the course, and continue to put on plays to raise money for its rent and upkeep.

E. Gordon Walker had won. She had given her finest performance. And to this day golfers, albeit unknowingly, continue to give her rave reviews.

E. Gordon Walker '00

The youngest member of her class and the school's only harpist, she was a member of the Red Headed Club. After graduation she often performed in charity fund raisers, and the Boston press dubbed her "the Rose of Arlington" (photo possibly taken after 1900).

Corinne Abercrombie '00

From Houston, Texas, she was Vice President of the Golf Club and had a leading role in *A Scrap of Paper*. The *Wellesley Magazine* of April 1900 described her as "an effective hit." Intriguingly, she was also Corresponding Secretary of the Matrimonial Bureau.

Wilhelmine Bayless '00

An avid member of the Golf Club, she was from Evanston, Illinois. A member of the Zoology Club and cox of her freshman year crew, her role in *A Scrap of Paper* prompted a reviewer to write that she was "a charming little maid."

Kathrina Storms '00

Editor-in-chief of the 1900 *Legenda*, she was from Evansville, Indiana, and played golf on the campus course. She also played basketball, chaired the Tree Day Committee and, with Bayless and Abercrombie, was a member of the Philosophy Club.

The New Wellesley Golf Club

Once the College trustees had agreed to the Wellesley Golf Club's plans, work on the new golf course started almost immediately. An opening date was set for October 1, 1900.

We do not know who laid out the new course, although an unnamed reporter in the *The Boston Evening Transcript* of July 25, 1900, observed that "A liberal interest has been taken in the laying out of the grounds, the committees have worked faithfully, and much friendly assistance has been furnished." As Arthur Hunnewell lived just down the road and had already laid out and built several golf courses—probably including the earlier campus course—he could easily have provided some experienced help. But the records are silent on this.

In July 1900, with the course still under construction, *The Boston Evening Transcript* reporter visited the site and filed a story describing each new hole in some detail, noting that "Golf experts pronounce the course one of the best of the many in this vicinity." (This article is reprinted in full in the Appendix.)

The course opened on schedule in October, and *Our Town* (a monthly newspaper and predecessor to *The Wellesley Townsman*) noted prophetically, "Golf has evidently come to stay for a long time." It went on to predict that the new club "bids fair to be one of the town's most successful organizations."

The November 1900 issue of *Our Town* included the following item in its "Wellesley College Notes" section: "OUT-DOOR INTERESTS. So uniformly fair has been the weather this autumn that out-door interests have come in for a goodly share of attention. Golf has perhaps been most popular of all the recreations, as the new course offers excellent opportunities for the playing of a considerable number of people. There is a large membership from the College in the new club, about twenty members of the faculty having joined and forty or fifty students. President Hazard has been made an honorary member of the Club, as has also Mr. Alphonse H. Hardy [the College treasurer], to whom the club is much indebted regarding the new links."

The new golf club also had members from the Dana Hall School which had close ties to the College.

Charles Dana of Nehoiden Farm

Charles Dana made a fortune in the East India trade and retired to the village of Wellesley in 1864 as a gentleman farmer. He purchased over 100 acres of land off Grove Street and called his holdings Nehoiden Farm. The farm's corn, potatoes, and hay were sold locally. A friend of the Durants in the 1860s, before they founded the College, Dana was active in the Congregational Church and served on its building committee. When a buyer couldn't be found for the church's old meeting house, he bought it and moved it to Nehoiden Farm. The Durants founded Dana Hall in 1881, the year Wellesley seceded from Needham, with the goal of better preparing students for the College. Henry Durant hired the first headmistress, and Dana donated the meeting house which was used by the school. The Durants named the school for Dana.

The Boston Evening Transcript reported in July 1900 that "Several members of the Wellesley Hills Golf Club have expressed a desire to join this club." The Wellesley Hills Golf Club would become the Wellesley Country Club in 1910.

BELOW: *This photo is of the golf team of the class of 1910. For many years, each class at the College had teams that competed on an intramural basis. At the time, ties were a popular fashion accessory.*

WELLESLEY GOLF CLUB—1900

The Wellesley Golf Club's course was built in the summer and fall of 1900 and was the successor to an earlier course that had been built across Washington Street on the main campus.

There were no pine trees separating the holes in 1900 and, as there is no way of knowing which large trees were in place at the time, none have been identified on the plan at right.

The Golf House is not shown because it was not built until 1903.

As with most courses of this era, the holes tended to be short, and there was only one tee per hole.

Original Hole No.	Current Number	1900 Length	2005 Length*
1	7	306	309
2	8	160	148
3	9	200	531
4	1	240	451
5	2	253	374
6	3	160	313
7	4	233	200
8	5	100	366
9	6	400	369
Total yardage		2,052	3,061

*From the back tees

ABOVE: *In 1900, town members would have gotten to the course by foot, on a bicycle (see page 32), or by horse, as there were still hardly any cars. This photo, taken at the Wellesley Hills railroad station in 1900, shows a train in the background, a dog cart, and a bicycle propped up against the pole at far right.*

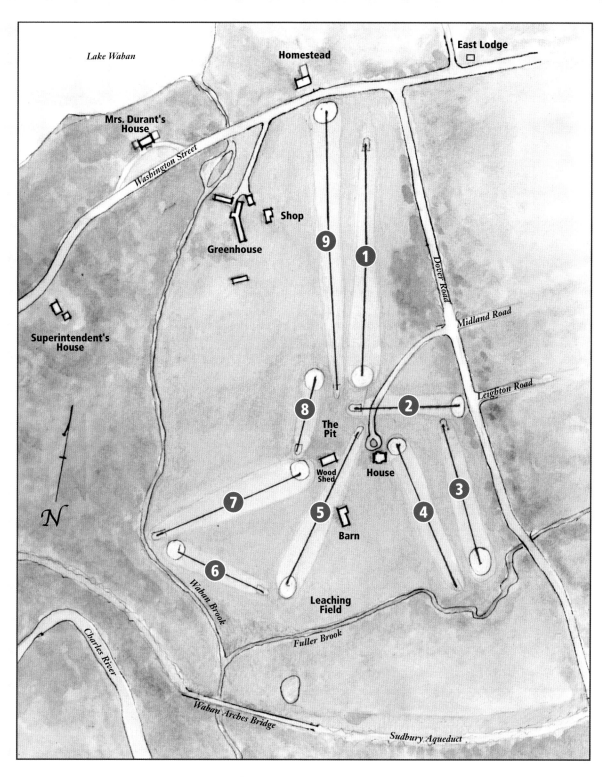

Golf Arrives in Massachusetts at the Hunnewell Estate

AT TOP: *The Oaks on Washington Street today. It was considerably modified in 1937.*

ABOVE: *The Oaks after it was rebuilt following a disastrous fire in 1891. The home of Arthur and Jane (Boit) Hunnewell, this 54-room mansion with 11 baths and servants' quarters was encircled by a six-hole golf course. The front yard contained the 3rd fairway and green.*

RIGHT: *Florence Boit arriving at the Wellesley railroad station at the time of her one visit to The Oaks in 1894. She came for a long stay and oversaw the creation of its golf course.*

FACING PAGE: *Golfing Hunnewell family members Robert Gould Shaw and Francis Williams Sargent on The Oaks course in 1901.*

The first private golf course in Massachusetts was built in 1892 at The Oaks on the Hunnewell Estate in Wellesley and endured for the better part of 50 years. Other than a temporary course that was laid out in Franklin Park in 1890, it was the first in the state.

The story of the six-hole Oaks golf course begins when Florence Boit and her father, Edward, visited Pau, a resort in the French Pyrénées. Edward loved to paint and, as it happens, he was the brother of Jane Boit, who had married Arthur Hunnewell. While Edward painted, Florence took up golf, probably at Pau-Billère on the banks of the River Gave in the tiny town of Pau. The course, the first on the Continent, was built in 1856 by the British army for its own use, and the area is still popular with the English.

Though American, the Boits lived mostly in Paris and Florence and often traveled within Europe. They also made trips to Boston where they had a town house on Beacon Hill. The one time that Florence visited her aunt and uncle in Wellesley, when she was 24, she stayed for a few months and brought her clubs along, presumably hoping to find a course nearby. While there were no courses in the state at that time, she most likely talked enthusiastically about the new game with her hosts, and it is known that she demonstrated how it was played. Arthur Hunnewell was keen on sports and had played baseball at Harvard. He and his brothers Walter and Henry and their brother-in-law Robert Gould Shaw soon built a course with the help of The Oaks' groundskeeper

Frederick Coles, and Florence (or Flourie, as she was called) supervised their work. The course made a circuit around the main house and is estimated to have been 2,025 yards. Four of the fairways crossed one another so that only a few golfers could safely play simultaneously. The tee boxes were raised, the greens were small, and there was only one sand trap. Part of the course went into The Pines, the adjoining Shaw estate.

In 1890, George Wright (of Wright & Ditson sporting goods fame) and four friends played a nine-hole round on a make-shift course he laid out in Franklin Park which lasted for a day. An ex-Nationals baseball player, he often demonstrated and promoted new games and sold sports equipment in his Boston store (see page 96).

Florence Boit's role in the history of golf in Massachusetts is important because she showed Arthur Hunnewell and his friend, Laurence Curtis, that golf was an engaging new sport. Curtis, after playing at The Oaks, wrote a letter to those in charge at The Country Club in Brookline (Curtis and the Hunnewells were members) requesting that a golf course be built on the grounds. Until then, The Country Club was a place where members could go for outdoor sports such as riding, croquet, and archery, but not golf. In November 1892, the following entry appeared in the minutes of the Executive Committee: "Voted:

In this well-known John Singer Sargent painting, The Daughters of Edward Darley Boit, *Florence Boit is second from left and, it is thought, was unhappy about having her picture painted.*

That Messrs. Arthur Hunnewell, Laurence Curtis and Robert Bacon be appointed as a Committee on Golf to lay out the course and spend the necessary amount up to $50."

In the spring of 1893, The Country Club's course opened with a match involving Arthur Hunnewell, Laurence Curtis, and George Cabot. Hunnewell was the first to tee off. His ball landed on the green and rolled right into the cup—a hole-in-one on the first shot, on the very first day! It was an auspicious beginning, although the gallery was reportedly disappointed when the feat was not repeated again that day.

For his pioneering role in golf, George Wright had a Donald Ross course named for him in Hyde Park, and Laurence Curtis became president of the USGA. But Florence Boit's role in golf history remains in relative obscurity. She has, however, received some public acclaim as the eldest of the four sisters in the John Singer Sargent painting, *The Daughters of Edward Darley Boit,* that hangs in Boston's Museum of Fine Arts. A friend of the Boits, Sargent did the painting in 1882. The sisters gave the painting to the museum in 1919, the year that Florence died.

Arthur Hunnewell

At Florence Boit's suggestion, he built the state's first private golf course in 1892, helped lay out the The Country Club course in 1893, played an exhibition match when it opened, and was probably the "Mr. Hunnewell" who laid out the golf course at Wellesley College in 1894.

Laurence Curtis

A friend of Arthur Hunnewell, he played The Oaks course in 1892 and was so taken with the game that he became instrumental in paving the way for The Country Club's first course. He was a founder of the USGA (representing TCC) and was its second president.

Stanley "Ted" Bishop

As a teenager in Natick, he caddied, shagged balls, and played golf at the Hunnewell course in the 1930s. Three-time Massachusetts State Amateur Champion and twice New England Amateur Champion, he became National Amateur Champion at Baltusrol in 1946.

Frank Hunnewell Williams

A direct descendant of Horatio Hollis Hunnewell, he lives at The Oaks. Williams is standing in what had been a fairway and is leaning against one of the trees that has grown in since the golf course fell into disuse in the early 1940s.

Caroline Hazard
President of Wellesley College from 1899 to 1910, she was a dedicated golfer, and "goes out frequently to play for an hour in the morning or afternoon." The members of the club made her an honorary member for her help in getting the course built.

Katharine Edwards
A professor of English at the College, she was an early devotée of golf and Vice President of the Wellesley Golf Club in 1900. Townsman Benjamin H. Sanborn was President, reflecting the early town-gown mix.

Early Club Organization

In 1903, the members of the Wellesley Golf Club, realizing that more formal arrangements were necessary, reorganized the club with new bylaws and officers. Representatives from the town, the College Department of Physical Training, and the College administration were appointed to consult on all matters related to golf at the now more official Wellesley Golf Club. This new administrative group became known as the Joint Committee.

For more than a century, 1903 has been considered the official year the club was founded. To be sure, it was the year when the College gained more control over the course and club through the Joint Committee—a group whose successor still meets once a year, during the winter, to recommend course improvements, set fees, and the like. This unique organization—a monument to town-gown relations—has remained in place and in working order for more than 100 years.

The affairs of the newly reorganized club did not go smoothly. Members found they couldn't make their lease payments and, in November 1906, the club was dissolved, although the students continued to play and golf was still a College sport. In April 1908, the Wellesley Golf Club was reorganized with the College in charge through the Joint Committee, and Wellesley residents were encouraged to join.

Over the next 16 years, the number of town memberships increased slowly, as did the annual fees. By the early 1920s, the number of town members in a given year was approximately 50, and the annual membership fee had risen to $25—from a low of $5 in 1904 when there were just 12 town members.

World War I

While some of the club's members may have left to serve in the armed forces, the war's impact on the course was marked by the appearance of a Victory Garden along the 6th* fairway, as Ward Fearnside recalls. At the College, several faculty members went overseas, and the students knitted clothing for the soldiers and raised money for war-related causes—including an ambulance that was sent to France in memory of Frances Warren Pershing '03, who had died in 1915 and whose husband General John "Black Jack" Pershing was the commander of the American Expeditionary Force.

* Throughout the text, holes are identified with today's numbers to minimize confusion, with the exception of the plans for 1900 and 1935.

AT LEFT: *The Golf Club House (now the Golf House) was built in 1903 when the 6th hole was the 9th, which made its location very convenient. When it was nearly finished its arrival was warmly welcomed by the* The College News, *which reported, "We may congratulate ourselves that we possess one of the prettiest and most satisfactory of the smaller club houses around Boston." The story went on to say that "for us golf players," the arrival of the clubhouse "will be a day of great rejoicing" because "There will be no more lugging of heavy bags and clubs back and forth from the course. . . ." Today the building is used primarily for events although clubs and balls are still stored here for the golf classes.*

BELOW LEFT: *From the very earliest years, the College retained golf pros to give lessons to the students.*

The College archives contain the 1917 bookkeeping entry that $235 was paid to Ray Ouimet for his services as a College golf instructor. Ray was the older brother of Francis Ouimet, the former caddie from Brookline who won the 1913 U.S. Open as an amateur at The Country Club in a breathtaking playoff.

Not long after his amazing victory, Ouimet heard about a Wellesley College golfer named Eleanor Russell '17 (possibly through his brother Ray) and invited her to be his partner in a Massachusetts pro-amateur tournament that they went on to win. Eleanor, who never weighed more than 105 pounds, had a 4 handicap and continued playing golf until she was 95. She married her high school sweetheart, Wendell Reycroft, was Connecticut amateur champion in 1925, played golf with Katherine Hepburn, and was a lifelong friend of Mayling Soong '17 (Madame Chiang Kai-Shek). Russell's father got Winchester golf pro Harry Bowler a job as golf instructor at the College. One day a week, Bowler gave individual 20-minute lessons to each of the students who had signed up for golf.

Because the College approached athletics "scientifically," Wellesley students were taught golf by experienced instructors from the very beginning in 1893 according to *The Boston Evening Transcript*, August 30, 1894. In 1899, there was the well-known golf professional Launcelot Cressy Servos. In 1902, there was a Mr. Howard of Harvard; in 1917, Ray Ouimet; and in 1937, Walter Thomas Howe of Wellesley Country Club.

We have little firsthand information about the early years at the course, but we do have a witness to some of its quirks and characteristics. As many neighborhood children do today, Ward Fearnside knew the course like the back of his hand. A Wellesley resident for most of his life, as a boy he lived on Upland Road, just a block from today's 7th tee.

Ray Ouimet

He was one of the early golf instructors at the College and was hired to give lessons in 1917. Four years earlier, his brother Francis won the U.S. Open at The Country Club in Brookline, galvanizing national interest in the game.

Eleanor Reycroft '17

She golfed at the College course, met Buffalo Bill Cody and Annie Oakley while she was out West on semester break, was at Fenway Park with her father on the day it opened in 1912, and met President Calvin Coolidge on her honeymoon.

Nehoiden: What's in a Name?

ABOVE: John Eliot Preaching to the Indians, *by Henry Oliver Walker, is one of four murals depicting early events in state history in Memorial Hall at the State House. The inscription reads: "I am about the work of the great God, and the great God is with me."*

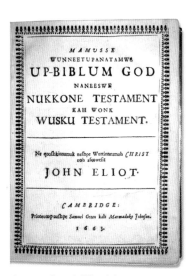

ABOVE: *It took Eliot 14 years to translate* The Bible *into Algonquian. This copy was published in 1663, and it is in the Special Collections at the Wellesley College library.*

Over the years, various stories have circulated about why the club is named Nehoiden. One has it that Nehoiden was a Native American princess, another that Nehoiden was a tribal chief. But of what tribe? And when? And why is the course named for this chief or his daughter?

As it turns out, William Nehoiden, a Native American, was born in 1635 in Unquity (in the Milton area) when the English were settling the Massachusetts Bay Colony. His father spoke English and acted as an intermediary with the settlers. As was common at the time, Nehoiden's name was spelled in a variety of ways, including Nahanton, Ahanton, and Hahaton.

Nehoiden's mother was a Pautuxet from the Lowell area, and his father was a Massachusett, one of the many Algonquian-speaking tribes who lived in eastern Massachusetts. Although the Massachusetts, Wampanoags, and Nipmucs were all of the Algonquian family, they were often on bad terms with one another.

Nehoiden was close to John Eliot, a dissenting minister who came to Massachusetts because he was deeply concerned for the Native Americans who knew nothing of Christianity. In 1651, Eliot established Natick—the first of the 14 "Praying Indian" villages he founded—as a safe haven for Native Americans on a 2,000-acre grant that ran from the falls on the Charles River in South Natick to Lake Waban.

Nehoiden often visited Eliot in Natick, played a key role in King Philip's War, was adept at land transactions, and signed his name to the deed that transferred Needham and much of Wellesley to the colonists in 1680. Nehoiden's name appears in many of the colony's early documents as he signed a number of deeds in the region and was the first Native American to get a divorce in the colonial court system.

Today there are still traces of Nehoiden's presence in the area. Newton, Needham, and Westwood all have a Nehoiden Street, there is a Nehoiden Glen apartment complex in Needham, and a Nahanton Park on the Charles River in Newton off Nahanton Street which is used as a summer camp. For a few weeks in 1881, the Wellesley Hills post office was renamed Nehoiden. Around this time, Westwood would have become Nahanton were it not for the objections of the town of Nahant. In the late 1800s, there was a Nehoiden Club in Wellesley (its building is now the Odd Fellows Hall on Central Street), whose members put

Needham resident N.C. Wyeth, who illustrated Treasure Island *and* Kidnapped, *did this romanticized drawing of Nehoiden in 1927.*

Nehoiden appears in the Needham town seal.

on talent shows. And in the 1980s, Needham celebrated Nehoiden Day.

It is not known exactly why the golf course was named for Nehoiden. The key is most likely Lake Waban, named in the 1850s for a Native American tribal leader whose name means "the wind" in Algonquian. One day, Eliot preached on a verse from Ezekiel wherein the spirit of the Lord is in the wind. Until this time Eliot hadn't had much luck getting the Native Americans interested in Christianity, but when Waban heard his name given such significance he was awestruck. From this point on, Eliot's mission became much more successful. The Native Americans gravitated to Christianity, and not long after, Natick was founded to provide them with a place to become more settled and study this new religion. Waban lived in Natick, and he and Nehoiden were interned on Deer Island during King Philip's War.

The golf course was probably named Nehoiden as a complement to nearby Lake Waban. After all, Nehoiden and Waban were contemporaries who lived in the same small area, were close to John Eliot, and played important roles in the early history of Natick, Wellesley, and the colony.

In 1919, Wellesley resident Ward Fearnside began cultivating a lifelong interest in hunting for golf balls—a passion he pursued for 85 years. He and his brother were also fascinated by what they concluded was a Native American campsite near what is now the practice green next to the 6th fairway. He recalls that when the vegetable garden on the left of the 6th fairway was plowed up, hundreds of flint chips and a few arrowheads would come to the surface (especially after a rain storm). The boys later mounted the arrowheads on boards that they gave to the College, but their whereabouts, sadly, are no longer known.

Fearnside reports that in the early years the College's maintenance area was essentially a large deposit of sand known as "the Pit." Because it was regularly excavated, it grew from a small hole in the ground to the large bowl that we know today. Eventually various buildings were added but not before the original green

for 5 and the original tees for 2, 6, and 8 were gobbled up and had to be relocated.

During this time, Fearnside recalls, Nehoiden's tees were often covered with sand because the most common method of teeing up was to take some wet sand from a bucket located near the tee, fashion a little pyramid, and then place the ball on top of it. However, sand build-up on the tees became something of a maintenance problem.

Fearnside remembers that in the early years the grass on the fairways was cut by a horse-drawn, three-unit reel mower, and the horse's hooves were covered with leather overshoes to prevent the grass from being dug up. A blacksmith shop was located just off Washington Street, on the short country lane that would become Service Drive, and Fearnside recalls that the blacksmith would shoe the reel-hauling horses, and as a sideline, sharpen the neighbors' lawn mower blades.

ABOVE: *During the First World War, student "farmerettes" did their bit by cultivating a College War Garden on a College-owned parcel across Central Street and bounded by Weston Road. Ward Fearnside remembers cabbages growing alongside the 6th fairway in 1919, and John Anderson's grandfather tended gardens on what is now the 5th fairway.*

Golf Course Names in the Region and King Philip's War

King Philip's War (1675–1678) resulted when the colonists tried to exert control over the Native Americans; it was exacerbated when the Native Americans realized that their "land sales" were permanent and not, as they had thought, easements. The Native Americans rose up in revolt and almost wiped out the colony. A number of area golf course names are distant echoes of this war.

Metacomet Country Club, Bristol, RI

The leader of the revolt was Metacomet, the Algonquian name for the man the English called King Philip. His story became an old New England legend—one that John Greenleaf Whittier memorialized in his poem *Metacom*. Metacomet lived in southeastern Massachusetts. He and his brother Wamsutta were sons of Massasoit, the Native American who ironically had been of great help to the Plymouth colonists.

Sassamon Trace Golf Course, Natick

John Sassamon was a Wampanoag who had been very close to Metacomet but left his tribe to become a teacher in Eliot's "Praying Indian" village of Natick. It is thought that Sassamon was murdered because he knew too much about Metacomet's plans, and it was his death that triggered King Philip's War.

Nehoiden Golf Club, Wellesley

William Nehoiden gave evidence as a witness to John Sassamon's murder by Metacomet's tribesmen. During the war, the settlers became distrustful of all Native Americans. Nehoiden, along with Waban and 200 Praying Indians from Natick, was interned on Deer Island in Boston Harbor, much to John Eliot's distress.

Montaup Country Club, Portsmouth, RI

Montaup—Anglicized as Mount Hope—was where

Metacomet had a hide-out. After Nehoiden was released from Deer Island in 1676, he is thought to have led the colonists to Montaup where they shot and killed Metacomet, whose death effectively ended the war, although skirmishes continued until 1678.

Wompanoag Golf Club, Swansea and Blue Hill Country Club, Canton

Metacomet was a Wampanoag and Nehoiden a Massachusett (Algonquian for a person who lives near the big hill—the one that we call Blue Hill).

Ponkapoag Golf Course, Canton

Ponkapoag in the Canton area was the name of one of the 14 Praying Indian villages that John Eliot founded in Massachusetts in the mid-1600s. Nehoiden lived in Ponkapoag after King Philip's War until his death in 1717.

Wayne Stiles—A Grand Plan

In the late 1920s, the Joint Committee finally got serious about upgrading the course layout and began looking into expansion plans that, in 1900, had been expected to take place "as soon as practicable"—which, as it turned out, was a quarter of a century later.

For reasons that are still unclear, a master plan for an 18-hole layout was drawn up by Wayne Stiles, the golf course architect who had redesigned the Wellesley Country Club in 1924 and who lived nearby in the Babson Park section of Needham. Stiles was a partner in the firm of Stiles and Van Kleek of Brookline and St. Petersburg, Florida, which designed Taconic Golf Club in Williamstown and Woodland Golf Club in Newton. Between 1924 and 1932 Stiles designed more than 60 golf courses in the northeast. An avid golfer, he had a single digit handicap and played out of Brae Burn in Newton, a fine Donald Ross course. In fact, no one other than Ross himself left a bigger mark on the New England golfing landscape than Wayne Stiles. Indeed, their ideas were similar, and a number of courses designed by Ross were given major redesigns by Stiles, including Wellesley Country Club.

His plans for Nehoiden are labeled "Wellesley College Golf Club" so it is possible that his involvement began before the name was changed to Nehoiden. It isn't clear whether he was paid for his work. No record can be found in the College archives of his remuneration by the Department of Hygiene and Physical

Wayne Stiles, golf course architect

Education or any other College group. Since he lived nearby, Stiles may well have known some committee members socially and advised them informally on some of the course changes made during this period.

The Stiles blueprint for Nehoiden (see Appendix) is in the Wellesley College archives and illustrates his plans for the property: 18 holes that utilized the existing course, the south side of the aqueduct, and an area west of Service Drive between the 5th fairway and Washington Street. Most of the club's original holes were eliminated by, or combined with, new holes. Stiles' large blueprint is actually three plans in one. It

shows the architect's 18-hole plan, the club's 9-hole layout as Stiles found it (presumably the original 1900 course), and some initial course changes enacted during 1928.

While the Stiles plan shows the extension of today's 9th and 1st holes, these are fairly obvious moves that could have been expected sooner or later (similar to the 2nd's move across Fuller Brook). However, the relocation of today's 8th green might have been less foreseeable, and we can probably credit Stiles with today's 5th, since an almost exact prototype of this hole is to be found in his 1927 plan.

The routing we know today has been in place for so long (more than 70 years) that it's hard to imagine just how differently the course played pre-Stiles, or how differently it would have played had his 18-hole vision been implemented. With all his changes, only one hole would have emerged in a form we would easily recognize: our 9th, which would have played as Stiles' 11th.

The Stiles vision included two holes for the other side of the Sudbury Aqueduct, on what was then known as the "Shaw Property"—one of these holes included a tee on top of the aqueduct itself. He also routed a number of holes between Waban Brook and Washington Street, including a graceful dogleg par-4 that finished across from the President's House. He imagined another striking hole that started near today's 9th green and played downhill, through the park-

ing lot, hugging the aqueduct on the left.

In some spots, Stiles combined existing course elements to make new ones. He proposed a dramatic combination of our 7th and 1st holes, which would have played as a 410-yard par-4 from the 7th tee to the 1st green.

While the end result might have been a somewhat tight 18-hole course, it would have added some challenges that are now lacking including a few long par-4s, some bona fide doglegs, and nine more holes.

Stiles is the closest Nehoiden ever came to having a professional course designer—something Williams College was the beneficiary of in 1927 when Stiles designed Taconic Golf Club.

Taconic is considered to be among the best golf courses in New England *and* among the top college courses in the country. Taconic has a relationship with Williamstown's residents that is quite similar to Nehoiden's relationship with the residents of Wellesley. And the two courses also have Will Reed in common—it was Reed who took charge of Nehoiden when he came to Wellesley in 1990 from Williams, where he had been president of Taconic.

As for any concerns that a Stiles course would have fit in with the landscaping philosophy of Wellesley College, GolfClubAtlas.com notes that the Taconic layout "enjoys a great naturalness with an absence of any heavy handedness by man."—the same objective the Durants had for Wellesley's landscaping.

THE 18-HOLE LAYOUT PROPOSED BY WAYNE STILES IN 1927

Wayne Stiles was a Needham resident who drew up an 18-hole layout for the Wellesley College course in 1927. Stiles was a distinguished golf course architect and partner in the design firm of Stiles and Van Kleek of Brookline and St. Petersburg, Florida.

Two of the holes (14 and 15) are simply indicated as being south of the Sudbury Aqueduct, and while we know their proposed distances, we do not know their layouts. It might be safe to assume that the 14th and 15th holes could have been more or less parallel to one another and the aqueduct.

Stiles designated the home that is now at 41 Service Drive as the clubhouse, and parking could have been in what is now the maintenance area.

As far as we know, Stiles is the only golf course architect who may have had an influence on Nehoiden. It may be that his plan gained some currency with the Joint Committee and could have influenced the layout of our present 5th hole and the location of our 8th green. Had his plan been implemented Nehoiden would have gained something that it still lacks: a few bona fide dogleg holes and some long par-4s.

The hole distances on the 6,065 yard course that Stiles designed are as follows:

Hole	Yards	Hole	Yards
1	360	10	140
2	150	11	480
3	400	12	375
4	390	13	130
5	315	14	435
6	225	15	415
7	345	16	350
8	355	17	440
9	410	18	340
Total	2,950		3,115

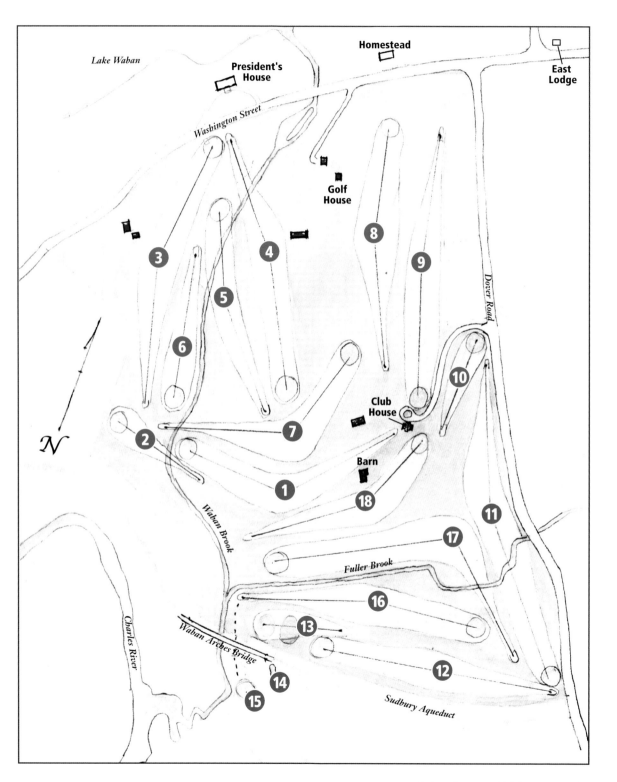

AT TOP: *This golf card was used around 1930 and features the new club emblem. See Appendix.*

ABOVE: *Through the 1920s, students held "pit parties" (often marshmallow and weenie roasts) "way out midst the golf links" (Wellesley Alumnae Magazine, December 1925). "The Pit" ultimately became the maintenance area. This photo was taken between 1918 and 1922; a hot dog on a stick can be seen at top right above the roofline of the house near the 2nd tee.*

AT RIGHT: *Dorothy Bolte was head of golf in 1927.*

After World War I

Having emerged from The Great War a bona fide if reluctant world power, America spent the 1920s making money, spending it, and cultivating a love for sports, which included building golf courses in record numbers. This was not only the age of Babe Ruth and Ty Cobb, but also of Bobby Jones and Walter Hagen, who played courses newly designed by such popular architects as Donald Ross and Wayne Stiles.

Greater Boston accounted for its fair share of this boom. Charles River Country Club in Newton (1921), Weston Golf Club (1923), and Wayland's Sandy Burr (1925) all opened in this heady era, which was also marked by the improvement of many earlier designs. Even The Country Club's course, considered good enough to host the U.S. Open in 1913, was given a complete redesign by William Flynn in 1922.

In town, the nine-hole Wellesley Country Club's golf course, originally a Donald Ross design, was deemed in need of modification. Interestingly enough, it was substantially redesigned by Wayne Stiles in 1924, according to golf course architect Geoffrey Cornish, who was retained to design the second nine in 1960.

With new construction and course renovation taking place all around them, the members and Joint Committee of the Wellesley Golf Club might have been disposed to reassess their layout. Some had even felt this way from the beginning. *The Boston Evening Transcript* reported in 1900 that that while the course was off to a good start, it would only be a matter of time before the 2,100 yard layout was lengthened and made more interesting with brooks, hazards, and a clubhouse.

Nehoiden Golf Club

In 1927 change was in the air. The Joint Committee finally decided to start making the long-anticipated changes to the holes as well as to change the name from the Wellesley Golf Club to Nehoiden Golf Club, although records in the archives inexplicably refer to it as Nehoiden as early as 1925. At a 1927 meeting, the Joint Committee—club President George A. Kearsley, Vice President Paul Babson, Secretary J. A. Symonds, and Mabel L. Cummings from the athletics department—approved the name change. They also signed off on the $3,879.15 annual budget and settled on a new membership fee: $25 per annum, though a husband and wife could play for $35. There were 60 members that year. Neither the minutes nor any College publications of the time explain why the name Nehoiden, in particular, was chosen.

The 1929 Rules and Regulations, however, are quite explicit about the importance of replacing divots and informed the members in no uncertain terms that the first infraction merited a warning, the second a fine, and the third, suspension.

The "New Course"

Each year throughout the 1920s and 1930s, a Wellesley College student was designated as head of golf. She kept records of attendance at golf classes and organized events and competitions. At the end of each season she submitted a detailed report. In 1929 the head of golf wrote that the "new course" was ready for play that year. The 1st, 2nd, 4th, 8th, and 9th holes had been

NEHOIDEN GOLF CLUB—1935

The Boston Evening Transcript optimistically reported in 1900 that "The course will be extended to add another four or five hundred yards as soon as practicable," but it wasn't until 1927 that the first serious changes were made. The same article states that: ". . . it is hoped that a clubhouse may be had at no very distant date," and by 1903 the Golf House was built next to what was then the 9th hole.

The following changes were made in the late 1920s and early 1930s:

- The 3rd and 4th holes (today's 1st and 9th) were lengthened by being extended across Fuller Brook.

- The 6th, 7th, and 8th "meadow holes" (today's 3rd, 4th, and 5th holes) were lengthened and redirected with the 8th (our 5th) taking the form that it still has.

Nehoiden is known for the daunting presence of several large trees, but in 1935 there were even more of these awkward obstructions, four of which—noted on the plan at right—were irreparably damaged by storms and are no longer standing.

 = Large oak or maple that is still in play

 = Large tree that was standing in 1935 but no longer exists

David Livingston and his 1931 Ford Phaeton. The car was bought in 1934 by his father, also a Nehoiden golfer, and it has been ferrying golfers to the course ever since. David has been a Nehoiden member since 2000, having "survived eight years on the waiting list."

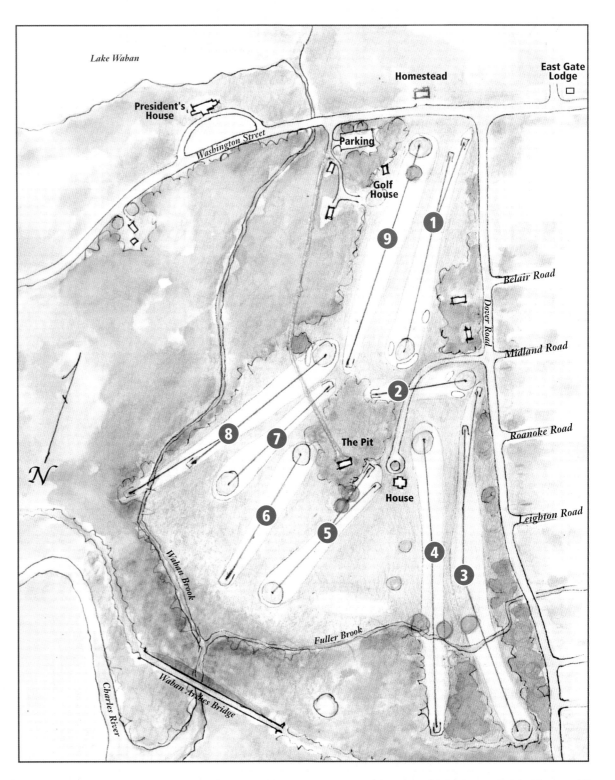

Our Place in History

The land that Nehoiden occupies has been owned by three noteworthy families since 1651: the Dewings, the Bullards, and the Durants. There is a document in the College archives that brings the three families together in the mid-1800s. It is a deed for 40 acres that Seth Dewing sold to Henry Durant and that was witnessed by Nathaniel Bullard. Before the Dewings, the land was occupied from time to time by the Native Americans who lived in the region, the Massachusetts, who would have moved in and out without leaving much of a trace, fishing in the lakes and rivers, and hunting in the woods.

John Eliot 1604–1690 "Apostle to the Indians"
John Eliot, whose spiritual vocation was to "save" the Native Americans, founded Natick as a Christian village in 1651. He built a sawmill on Waban Brook to provide the Native Americans with a more settled way of life. The sawmill was destroyed by fearful settlers while the Native Americans, including Nehoiden, were interned on Deer Island during King Philip's War (1675–1678).

Andrew Dewing 1616–1680
He received a grant of the "Natick Dividend" from Dedham in 1651 and was the first settler to build a house in what is now Wellesley in 1672. His acreage most likely included the site of the golf course; Fuller Brook, where it runs though the course, was then called Dewing's Brook. At first Dewing was a town fence viewer charged with confirming fence locations and their state of repair as roaming livestock were a problem. Later he became a selectman and then a captain in the militia and was put in charge of the Native Americans when they returned from Deer Island in 1676. In the 1700s, Dewing descendants sold a portion of their land to the Bullards, but as old records are not always good or even available, it is impossible to be precise.

Bullard's Tavern and the Call to Arms in 1775
When word was brought to the Minutemen of West Needham (now Wellesley) that the British had landed, it came to the center of village life—Bullard's Tavern—on April 19, 1775. The area's Minutemen rallied at the tavern, then headed off to Arlington, arriving just in time to attack the Redcoats as they were retreating.

The Durants and Wellesley College
Cousins of the Hunnewells, the Durants bought the Bullard farm and a number of adjacent parcels during the mid- to late 1800s to assemble their 300-acre Wellesley estate. When the Durants first moved to Wellesley, they lived at Homestead, originally a Bullard farmhouse. When their son died in 1864, the Durants were devastated. Henry became deeply religious, and after much thought, they decided to open a women's college—a very forward-looking thing to do at the time—and they did so with the same sort of fervent conviction that inspired John Eliot to establish Natick for the Native Americans.

The Durants' plans for a college were formalized in 1870, and the doors opened in 1875. For many years, the main entrance gate was located on Washington Street near the site of Bullard's Tavern. East Lodge and the gates still exist, but the entrance is now across from the 6th green.

Golf Course at The Oaks, Hunnewell Estate, 1892
The first private golf course in Massachusetts was built at The Oaks by Arthur Hunnewell in 1892. Private courses were not uncommon at the time and were to be found on estates of the Cabots (Brookline), Rockefellers (Pocantico Hills, NY), and Vanderbilts (Asheville, NC), among others.

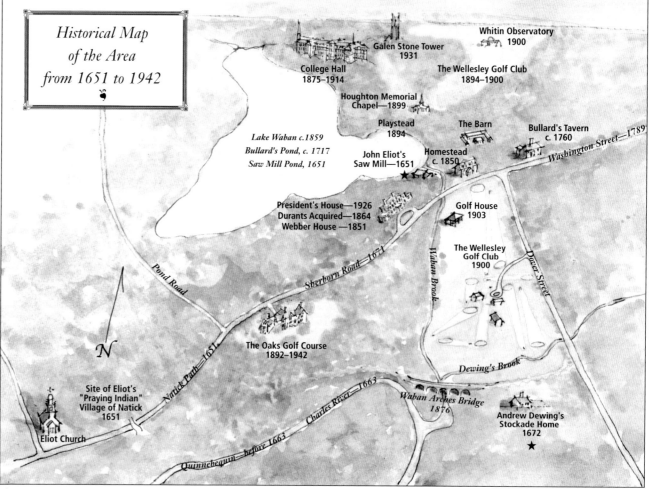

Historical Map of the Area from 1651 to 1942

★ = Location approximate

lengthened, and new hazards had been added. A practice fairway had been opened beside the 6th fairway and was in good condition. Par on the course was now 36 for men and 40 for women. What had been 2,100 yards was now up to roughly 2,800 yards. The head of golf concluded, "This year the course seems to be in better condition than ever, and the new 8th green [the current 5th] is a big improvement. There are a number of changes to be made in the course next year, and our course ought to be better yet."

Following the name change and the expansion in 1927-29, the life of Nehoiden Golf Club appeared to be relatively uneventful. Club records from 1930 include memos regarding the lease of horses, a tractor, a truck, and a Wilford shovel—an earth-moving device. Use of this particular machinery tells us that course improvements continued apace. The following year, the Joint Committee authorized improvements to the 5th green, which had been the source of committee consternation since 1929. At the 1931 meeting, Secretary Symonds was authorized to invite Bobby Jones and Francis Ouimet to play an exhibition match at Nehoiden to benefit the Wellesley College Swimming Pool Fund. As Francis Ouimet was living in Wellesley at the time and his brother Ray had taught at the College, this idea was not as far-fetched as it might seem now. But the match never took place as far as we can tell. In 1931, the committee instituted a policy permitting caddies—providing that the member who brought the caddie to the course took him home at the end of the round. This would have revived an older custom, as Katharine Lee Bates had noted in her diary of November 2, 1900, that she had used one Willie Buckley as her caddy.

The Great Depression

Even though the College and Nehoiden managed to skirt the serious economic hardships of the Depression, beginning in 1933 we see evidence of economizing. Though greenskeeper Robert MacBey was authorized to make improvements to "traps, rough, tees and so

forth," the Joint Committee's notes also detail the exact cost of renting grounds equipment: Roseman tractor, 65 cents per hour; Toro lawn mower, 30 cents; Penn Quint lawn mower, 65 cents. The club was closely watching its expenditures, although it had always been in the habit of doing so.

By the 1936 annual meeting, membership had fallen to 80, a fact the Joint Committee partly attributed to a reduction of fees at Wellesley Country Club and the competition from the new Leo J. Martin Memorial Golf Club in Weston.

A year later, the Joint Committee voted to drop its membership in the MGA, a move that saved the club $80. At this same 1937 meeting, letters from members

ABOVE: *During the 1920s and 1930s, Wellesley College received a number of major donations that enabled it to add dramatically to the campus. Galen Stone Tower was built in 1931 thanks to a contribution by Galen L. Stone, a successful Boston banker. This Wellesley landmark is visible from several locations on the golf course.*

complaining about the deteriorating playing conditions were also discussed.

Hundreds of private golf courses, which typically catered to the wealthy, were abandoned during the 1930s or became municipal or public operations. Although the National Golf Foundation's statistics indicate that 1,040 courses (or roughly 20 percent) closed their doors during this period, new courses, mostly public, were being built. It was during this time that public golf got its real start. Interestingly, the George Wright Golf Club in Hyde Park, a Donald Ross design, was built as a Works Progress Administration (WPA) project during the Depression.

Nehoiden survived the 1930s intact, and greenskeeper MacBey kept the place in decent shape, displaying the sort of discipline and resourcefulness which helped him become the town's chief of police during the mid-1950s.

World War II

By 1941, the club's membership had risen to 135, and the club had the money to undertake capital improvements—including the creation of the large bunker that guards the 5th green (the brainchild of the well-regarded Frank Scheufele, who became the College's Supervisor of Grounds from 1953 to 1959).

With America's entry into the war younger members left to serve in the armed forces, and Victory Gardens once again made their appearance. Long-time member Mary Rich—a 1955 graduate of the College—remembers hearing that plots near the 6th and 7th fairways were used for growing potatoes. Wellesley's president, Mildred McAfee, became the first woman commissioned by the Navy and director of the newly created Women's Reserve of the U.S. Naval Reserves (the WAVES), for which she received the Distinguished

AT LEFT: *Pine trees were planted between the fairways in the 1950s by course superintendent Bill Donovan and his assistant Frank Kane (inset photo). Donovan, who joined the Wellesley Police Department in 1962, is now retired and lives in Natick.*

Service Medal (awarded by the Secretary of the Navy) and appeared on the cover of *Time*.

In 1943, when club membership had dropped to just 67, special membership privileges were extended to clergy of the town's churches, and 50 more memberships were made available to town employees (now including public school teachers), with no waiting list requirements. Employees and retired employees of Wellesley College could also join, with reduced fees and no waiting list. The war would end, but these special memberships remained and furthered Nehoiden's unique membership mix that we still enjoy.

After World War II

Postwar, the golf community we recognize today began to emerge. The Men's Group was formed, and several familiar names like Fred Nolan, Bill Hudson, and Joe Sims appeared.

"My memories of Nehoiden date from 1946 when I was liberated from the Navy," recalls Nolan. He grew up in Boston, but his family had a summer place in Wellesley that Nolan eventually made his year-round home.

Joe Sims started working for the College in the early 1950s, pruning trees, and soon joined Nehoiden. He later worked in the sheet metal shop, served as the Wellesley College union president, and he began the College employee golf tournament so that College personnel could get to know one another better. Bev Schiavone in the controller's office helped expand the outing, which had begun with the grounds crew, to include all of the employees of the College.

Sims points out that the water level in Fuller Brook in the 1950s was much higher, and hence the brook was quite a bit wider—in fact, the second level of its banks was under water.

During the early 1950s, the man who tended to the brook, and the golf course all around it, was head greenskeeper Louis Payson.

Dues were increased in 1952, and a year later the Joint Committee considered rejoining the MGA. Indeed, Nehoiden's MGA membership had lapsed for 16 years, but the matter was tabled. By one reckoning, Nehoiden turned 50 in 1953, but there is no mention of an anniversary or celebration of any sort in the minutes or archives.

At the same 1953 meeting, it was announced that head greenskeeper Louis Payson would be leaving his

ABOVE: *Fred Nolan, Leo Nolan, Bernie Garron, and Herb Ireland c. 1947 are shown behind Fred Nolan's bridge table which was used for record keeping at a tournament that began on the 7th hole (then the 1st).*

Scott Birney

During World War II he served as a seaman aboard the battleship *New York* in the Pacific. A member since 1968, he is a professor of astronomy emeritus at the College.
Best Shot: Chipping in for a par on the 9th.
Favorite Hole: The 6th

Eleanor Webster '42

She first studied cryptography but felt she could better help the war effort by becoming a chemist and welding B-29 parts as a volunteer. She was a chemistry professor at Wellesley from 1952 to 1985 and admits to having always loved Nehoiden.

John Anderson

He was in the Marines 1944–45 in the ground crew on Guam at a base for night fighters where disabled B-29s were sent to crash land. In the 1946 colorized photo above, he is a recently discharged corporal. He often visited his aunt and uncle in the house by the 2nd tee. He was a Wellesley fireman for 32 years.

Inge Reinhard

She sang and entertained the troops at the USO in New York City during the 1940s (where her most popular request was *Lily Marlene*). After the war, she signed with MCA, then sang in Paris, at the Blue Angel in NYC, and on Jack Paar's *Tonight Show*. She has always been a Women's Group enthusiast.

post. Stewart Cornell replaced Payson at Nehoiden and was given a new title: General Foreman of Grounds. In a letter from Wellesley College Business Manager Irwin K. French, Cornell was urged to continue to be "fair and considerate" in dealing with town members.

In 1954, Nehoiden's Joint Committee finally submitted its new bylaws to the MGA, paving the way for club membership beginning that spring. Official handicaps and legitimacy (in the eyes of some) had been restored to Nehoiden Golf Club.

Postwar Projects

In 1954 there seemed to be a change in the attitude of Nehoiden members toward their golf course. Building projects were proposed in earnest and without interruption for the next eight years. Some were executed, some were not. In May, for example, a request was made for a larger practice area for the club. This was never enacted, and Nehoiden's irons-only practice area is still located between the 1st and 2nd fairways.

In February 1954, however, the Joint Committee had solicited estimates for rebuilding the bridge on the 9th, a job done that summer. In 1955, the committee discussed expanding the course water supply, repairing other bridges, relocating the 2nd and 6th greens, improving the 6th and 7th fairways, and constructing storm shelters. The 2nd and 6th greens were not relocated but were regrassed that very summer, using sod from the club's own nursery, then located between the 3rd and 4th fairways.

Amid the talk of building and improving, club life continued apace at Nehoiden. In June 1954, a conscientious member complained to the Joint Committee that no one had approached her to request payment for her guest and that not enough effort was being made to collect such fees. Local rules were changed that year: ladies would get a free lift if their drive on the 1st hole went into Fuller Brook.

The mid-1950s saw universal rule changes that would alter play at Nehoiden drastically and, it appeared, forever. The story of Nehoiden's ubiquitous

150-Yard Marker Bushes

In the 1960s, Don Gardner, below, and Pat Murphy felt that it was high time that the course had 150-yard markers. They set about remedying the situation by purchasing 14 bushes at their own expense and planting them on the course. The College union filed a grievance that this was union work, but the dispute was apparently settled amicably. While three of these marker bushes are still in evidence on the 2nd, 6th, and 7th holes, the others have disappeared. Their use as distance guides diminished when the course was remeasured and they were no longer accurate. The bush that is on the right side of the 2nd fairway, pictured here with Don, has often been taken for the 150-yard marker for the 3rd— with dire results. But it is still useful today as it can be used as the 132-yard marker to the center of the 3rd green. During 2003, a few replacement bushes began to crop up on the 2nd and 3rd fairways.

FACING PAGE: *The 2nd green almost made it across Fuller Brook in 1955. It was finally moved and ready for play in 1962.*

AT LEFT: *A College student putts on the 5th green during the spring, some time in the 1950s judging by the cinch belt and Bermuda shorts.*

The History of Nehoiden • **23**

ABOVE: *The Wellesley College Club opened in 1963 and became very popular. The parking lot across Washington Street soon became overcrowded, and Nehoiden got a new lot and changed its hole numbering.*

out-of-bounds markers involves Tom Howe, a member of the Men's Group in the 1950s. His father was the pro at Wellesley Country Club and gave golf lessons at Nehoiden during the late 1930s. Before the evergreens lined most of the fairways, Nehoiden had several holes for which a shot into the parallel fairway would constitute sound strategy, although there must have been some concern for the safety of other players. Apparently, Howe didn't hit a long ball and saw other, stronger players at Nehoiden hitting long drives onto adjacent fairways, which he considered an unfair advantage.

Howe obtained authority from the Men's Group to put in rows of out-of-bounds stakes—first on those holes where it was justified, but eventually on all holes with only minor exceptions.

Current members often justify the number of out-of-bounds at Nehoiden as a way to make what is a relatively short course just that much more difficult. Take the 313-yard 3rd hole: on most courses a drive into the opposing 2nd fairway wouldn't be OB but at Nehoiden it is. Today the pine trees separating the fairways would make the task of getting back that much harder—if it were allowable, which it isn't, thanks to Tom Howe.

The mid-1950s also saw a gradual change in the number of golfers who played, and sought to play, at Nehoiden. In 1954, the club voted to continue offering memberships to teachers in the Wellesley public schools, reaffirming a policy which had apparently been called into question. A few years later, Joint Committee minutes indicate that the subject of memberships for town employees came up again. It was decided that four complimentary passes would be offered annually to the town police and fire departments, which surely must have pleased Robert MacBey, Nehoiden's former greenskeeper, when he became the Town of Wellesley's chief of police. He was an excellent golfer, according to member Bill Hudson.

The decade also saw an explosion of tree planting, mostly pines. Today it is hard to imagine what the course would be like without these barriers. Course superintendent Bill Donovan (1957–62) succeeded Cornell and was responsible for much of this arboreal enterprise. It was he who planted the rows of pines alongside the fairways. Originally, Donovan says, he planned a row between 6 and 7, but College officials objected, saying it restricted the students' practice area. Perhaps it was thought that these pines would grow, and eventually Tom Howe's out-of-bounds scheme could be abandoned or curbed. (We're closing in on 50 years, and some are still waiting.)

Modern Times

Heavy snows during the winter of 1962 demolished the boat house on Lake Waban, destroying all of the College's crew shells. Other physical education programs took up the slack, and more golf classes were scheduled. This, combined with the fact that Nehoiden now had more members than ever, meant the course was accommodating much more play.

This was the situation when Tony Oteri became Nehoiden's greenskeeper in 1963 and moved his family into the house at 41 Service Drive beside the 2nd tee. Oteri, who would preside over the course's well-being

Robert Schneider

College business manager and vice president, his chief concern about grass cutting at Nehoiden was that everything should look good from Washington Street and Dover Road. The Schneider Student Center was named for him in 1970.

Robert MacBey

He served as Nehoiden's grounds superintendent during the 1930s and became chief of police for the Town of Wellesley in 1954. He played golf regularly at Nehoiden both as a Wellesley employee and police chief.

Mary Norton Rich '55

Admits that she applied to Wellesley because of its golf course, but stressed class size in her application. Still an active member, she remembers the 8th as being a much tougher hole when an embankment guarded the green.

Margaret Clapp '30

A Pulitzer Prize winning historian, she was president of Wellesley from 1949 to 1966, and she personally intervened in the move of Nehoiden's parking lot in 1964 to its present location (when the current president was a student).

for the next 33 years, arrived at Nehoiden from The Country Club in Brookline, where he had served on the maintenance team. Always a fine player (he won Nehoiden's club championship in 1978), Oteri sometimes gave evening lessons to members, in addition to his greenskeeping duties.

When Oteri arrived, Nehoiden was not especially green. In fact, in 1963, the College Business Manager, Robert Schneider (who lived on Dover Road) sent a memo to the Physical Plant Department directing that Nehoiden's fairways should not be too generously watered. Less water would mean less mowing, thus saving money on both counts. "However," Schneider added, "be sure to keep things looking nice on Dover Road and Washington Street."

Nehoiden's irrigation at that time involved hand-watering with a system of hoses. Directives from the College business manager aside, the fairways and rough already went largely unirrigated. "We had access to some water," Oteri recalls, "but it was mainly distributed through the hoses and portable sprinklers. With some irrigation, I always knew we could have a nice lit-

tle golf course. But we couldn't do much with the fairways until that happened." Though it remained a maintenance staff priority, comprehensive irrigation would not become a reality at Nehoiden for another 30 years.

With capital improvements and increases in membership, Nehoiden Golf Club was changing. Accustomed as we are today to playing a course with 800 members, we might chuckle at the idea of 225 members making the course feel crowded. But during the 1960s, members may have felt that way, and the growing membership even began to impinge on some of Nehoiden's neighbors.

Changing the Hole Numbers

When the golf course was built in 1900, there was no need for a parking lot since there were very few automobiles. Presumably the town members either walked to the course or came by horse and carriage. But as the automobile became more and more prevalent, town members began parking their cars in the most logical spot available: along Dover Road near what was then

Joe Sims
First played Nehoiden in the early 1950s when he worked on the grounds crew. He became Wellesley College union president and initiated the College employee golf tournament. He still plays at Nehoiden though he now lives in New Hampshire.

the opening hole on the golf course (today's 7th).

The side of the road seemed to work fine for parking until 1927. In August of that year, *The Wellesley Townsman* reported that neighbors and others objected to the 20 to 30 cars usually parked near the opening hole because they "marred the beauty of the street." The *Townsman* noted that the "College authorities . . . wishing to reciprocate the many favors of the Town of Wellesley" responded by building a parking lot adjacent to the 6th green and directly across from what would become the Wellesley College Club.

For a number of years the parking problem subsided, but as the membership grew, the new parking lot overflowed on Saturdays and Sundays when the course was most crowded. Golfers again resorted to parking along Dover Road to be close to the opening hole. Early on these weekend mornings, there was often loud banter among the players while they waited to tee off.

In 1963 a new ingredient was added to the mix: The Wellesley College Club was built and quickly became a popular place for lunches, dinners, and meetings. The overflow from the College Club's parking lot went into the Nehoiden lot, and parking once again became a problem.

In 1964, the town's Board of Selectmen took charge of the matter. With input from Wellesley College President Margaret Clapp and Chairman of the Board of Trustees John Quarles, the selectmen decreed that a dedicated Nehoiden Golf Club parking lot should be built where it is today, off Dover Road. As a result, the original 1st hole would become the new 7th, the 4th would become the new 1st, and the rest of the holes would be renumbered accordingly.

The entrance to the parking lot was to be opposite Ingraham Road. Neighbors near the proposed entrance objected, but the selectmen stuck to their guns. The new parking arrangement worked out well. The neighbors were happy (on one end of Dover Road, at any rate); the patrons of the Wellesley College Club were happy; and the golfers were happy.

From a golfing perspective, the entrance road

(paved over in 1966 at a cost of $1,154) that was laid across the new 9th fairway hardly affected play. And the new routing now separated Nehoiden's two longest holes. Instead of back-to-back, they now played first and last.

Waiting Lists and Memberships

In 1966, the waiting list had ballooned to 521—a figure that we can attribute to the growth of Wellesley's population and to golf's growing popularity during the 1960s. But some of this interest was also probably due to the quality and spirit of Nehoiden's golf course and club.

From that period to the present day, Nehoiden has been obliged to walk a fine line between meeting its financial needs and overcrowding the golf course, as well as balancing the interests of town members and the golf program at the College. The Joint Committee has done remarkably well, but it has not always been easy. At the 1967 meeting, concern was raised over the large number of people on the waiting list. A plan was instituted whereby a person on the waiting list could be paired with a member and play regularly as a guest of that member. In 1971, it was decided that the top 25 people on the waiting list would be offered weekday-only memberships.

By 1979 the waiting list had dropped almost to zero, and an advertisement soliciting membership was placed in *The Wellesley Townsman*. It seemed to work, because the waiting list quickly grew back—but it also seemed that not all of those on the list intended to join. The committee therefore devised a new approach: persons who reached the top of the list and declined went to the bottom and would have to work their way back up. There was also a $15 fee for this reassessment, and if there was a second refusal to join, the person was dropped from the list altogether.

Perhaps the biggest change is the number of golfers this 100-year-plus golf course has absorbed and continues to accommodate today.

Jon Hamilton
Wellesley High School golf coach and history teacher, he uses Nehoiden for team try-outs, practice, and tournaments in September and Wellesley Country Club in October.
Handicap: 4 **Best Shot:** Hole-in-one on the 4th

Norm Gavoni
Grew up in Wellesley, caddied at Wellesley Country Club, and played golf at Leo J. Martin. A professor of marketing at Babson College, he has served on Nehoiden's Joint Committee.
Likes Best: The variety of people at the club

Tony Vahey
He comes from a golfing family and has officiated at MGA tournaments. Once golfed with Ted Bishop, the 1949 National Amateur champion who played the Hunnewell course in the 1930s.

FACING PAGE: *The Wellesley High School golf team practices and plays tournaments at Nehoiden during September each year.*

AT TOP: *Frost covers the 9th fairway in the fall.*

ABOVE: *The bridge over Fuller Brook on the 9th hole replaced a wooden structure in 2000 and can comfortably accommodate any number of golfers. When its concrete pilings and steel girders were being put in place (to meet state requirements), there was some speculation that the National Guard might use it for tank maneuvers.*

Course Improvements

In 1967, Tony Oteri was offered the job of head greenskeeper at Blue Hill Country Club, a private course in Canton. To keep him, the College promoted him and put him in charge of all College grounds, including the golf course and the motor pool. Oteri and his new greenskeeper, Joe Catanzaro, soon set about improving Nehoiden's irrigation. In 1968, they successfully convinced the Joint Committee to install single-row irrigation on the 6th and 7th holes.

It did not happen right away, but in 1970 the new system (with its pump house beside the Golf House) was activated. "There's a reason why we did these holes first," Oteri says. "They were the closest to the water

line from the main campus that supplied all the houses on Service Drive, the motor pool, and the maintenance buildings."

"There were irrigation plans for the rest of the course, but a series of people arrived at the College who were not particularly supportive of the idea." Oteri adds, "Finally Vice President Will Reed arrived. He was a serious golfer, knew something about golf course management, and supported the idea."

In addition to the irrigation work on the 6th and 7th, a portion of the maintenance building closest to the 3rd green was modified in 1968 to provide rest rooms and a shelter, and more recently a vending machine was added. At the January 1969 meeting, Oteri was authorized to add a new and larger practice green next to the Golf House, and by October it was in place.

Nehoiden also braced itself for one change that never took place. In 1968, the town publicly discussed the idea of widening Route 16 enough to claim Nehoiden's signature 6th green. The Joint Committee decided that, should this come to pass, the green would be moved up the hill and the hole converted to a par-3. To maintain the course par of 36, the 4th hole would be lengthened to a par-4, playing to a putting surface located across Waban Brook. However, Washington Street was never widened, and the 6th green was saved.

In 1978, in a gesture that spoke eloquently to the longstanding cooperation between College and golf club, Nehoiden members became eligible to join the Wellesley College Club.

Since 1980, there have been many more improvements, alliances, and events at Nehoiden. Some we might recall, while others may have received little notice; still others we already take for granted.

For years, the Wellesley High School golf team has held its practices and Bay State League matches at Nehoiden. In 1979, the club granted the high school ski team permission to use the property for its cross-country training and meets. Two years later, Wellesley College reached an agreement permitting MIT students to play the golf course and in exchange, Wellesley students could use MIT's skating rink in Cambridge.

In 1983, the town upgraded the sewer pipes that had been connected to the College's system in 1958. As in the 1950s when Fuller Brook was rerouted, play was interrupted on the 1st, 2nd, and 9th holes.

More Support for Nehoiden

In any organization, it helps to have an advocate in high places. For Nehoiden, that person was Will Reed, who became the Wellesley College vice president for finance and administration in January 1990. He had held a similar position at Williams College and served as president

of the college-owned Taconic Golf Club.

Taconic is considered one of the top golf layouts in the state and, coincidentally, a Wayne Stiles design masterpiece. But Reed had another interesting golfing credential. He grew up in Bexley, Ohio, a suburb of Columbus, and was captain of its high school golf team. Bexley's arch rival was Upper Arlington High School, and the captain of their team was a young fellow named Jack Nicklaus. As Reed puts it, he has probably been beaten by Nicklaus head-to-head more times than anyone else on the planet.

Arriving at a time when women's athletics nationwide were getting more and more attention, Reed saw clearly that Wellesley College's golf facility was not in good shape. The problem was that not enough money was being spent on maintaining and upgrading. Tony Oteri was doing an excellent job with what he had, but he simply did not have enough staff or proper equipment to improve the course.

Because club dues were so low, Nehoiden had always been recognized locally as the "best value in golf," while the course was a wonderful way to maintain good relations with the town. So the trick was to increase the dues fast enough to make a difference in the course quality, but not so fast as to alienate the membership. With the Joint Committee, Reed decided to increase the annual dues by 10 percent for several years. The pledge was that the increased revenue would be spent directly on the course. Tony Oteri then drew up a prioritized list of projects, and Nehoiden began to show signs of improvement.

When Tony retired in 1996, he was replaced by Patrick Willoughby, who continued to improve the course. A number of expensive major capital projects were addressed including replacing the bridges on the 1st and 9th holes. New mowers were purchased for the fairways and greens, and the installation of the automatic watering system that Tony Oteri had initiated was completed. In a sense, the entire effort during the 1990s should be viewed as the final phase of the modernization program that had begun in the late 1920s. Nehoiden members now enjoy the results of

Tony Oteri
Longtime superintendent of Nehoiden, Tony Oteri arrived in 1963 and for many years lived with his family in the house by the 2nd tee. He became Wellesley's assistant director of physical plant, was a very good golfer, and usually had a single-digit handicap. **Club Champion:** 1978

Will Reed
Vice president for finance and administration at Wellesley 1990-2000 and VP of the College in 2000–2002. He lived in Nehoiden House overlooking the 1st fairway, was behind many of the course improvements, and now lives in New Hampshire. **Handicap:** Ranged from 12 to 15

Pam Kuong
Joined in 2004 after spending eight and half years on the waiting list. She took up golf ten years ago and enjoys the friendliness of Nehoiden's membership. She is a commercial lending officer with Bank of America. **Best Round:** 77 **Women's Open Champion:** 2004

these efforts, and Wellesley College offers a vastly improved athletic facility for its students.

In 1998, yardage markers were placed on sprinkler heads, metal spikes were banned, and the parking lot was improved with granite curbing and plantings. An attractive entrance shed with notice boards was built in 1999, and a portable sanitary facility was provided near the 1st tee. Improvements were made to the practice area where PGA teaching professional Ken Bellerose has been giving lessons since 1996: new tee boxes were built in 2001, an automated device was acquired for picking up balls, and in 2003 range balls were available through a mechanized dispenser at a dollar per bucket.

A milestone was reached in the fall of 2001 when the College hosted its first intercollegiate golf tournament, the Wellesley Invitational—surely the most important competition in Nehoiden's history. It has been an unmitigated success ever since, and Wellesley's new golf team has fared well, coming in first in both the spring and fall tournaments in 2004 ahead of teams from Mount Holyoke, Babson, Bowdoin, and Williams.

MGA Rating of the Course

At the beginning of the 2002 season, the Nehoiden scorecard was revised. Jim Donahue, a longtime club member and now golf course coordinator at Wellesley College, was put in charge of the project. Yardages on the 1st and 5th holes were finally amended to recognize the forward tees built years before. Since individual hole handicaps are determined by a club's membership, Donahue polled many of the members and adjusted the handicaps on the new scorecards which also feature a photo he took (and is the same view used for the cover of this book).

Many members have wondered how difficult Nehoiden is compared with other courses in the area. As it turns out, the MGA has a detailed system of evaluating all the state's courses. A course rating is defined by what par should be for a scratch player. The second number, slope, is the relative difficulty for someone

playing the course for the first time. According to the MGA, the average slope for all its courses in Massachusetts is 113.

Some Nehoiden members thought the club's MGA slope rating was too high, so Donahue requested that the MGA do a new survey. The results were as follows: from the blue tees 70.0/126, from the whites 69.2/125, and from the reds 68.4/125. This was a slight increase in difficulty compared to the prior survey, an unexpected result. Interestingly, the MGA did not take into consideration the out-of-bounds in parallel fairways, a local rule that probably challenges guests more than it does the members.

The overall interpretation is that the MGA evaluation is pretty fair. For a really good player the relatively wide and trap-free fairways make driving the ball a straightforward proposition. Approach shots to greens that are small and well-guarded then require only short irons. The course is literally there for the taking; hence its below-par rating (par from the white tees is 72 but its sub-par rating is 68.2). It is, perhaps, surprising that Senior PGA touring pro Allen Doyle shot a 66 at Nehoiden a few years ago; although, according to his host and college roommate, Richie Howard, his score could easily have been lower because he wasn't having a good day.

Obviously, the average guest at Nehoiden will have more difficulty than a touring pro, but the MGA survey results indicate that when the many and various individual factors are taken into consideration, Nehoiden is particularly difficult for someone who doesn't know the course, especially the blind or elevated greens on the 1st, 5th, 6th, and 9th holes.

Member Hal Phillips occasionally has a guest at Nehoiden who has played golf all over the world and whose assessment would seem to underscore the MGA's conclusion. The guest said, after one of their rounds, "Nehoiden really doesn't look that hard, but if you're not careful it can really get nasty."

NEHOIDEN GOLF CLUB—2005

The course as we know it today has gone through a number of changes since 1935:

- The pine trees that separate most of the fairways were planted during the mid-1950s.

- Fuller Brook was straightened in the 1950s to reduce flooding and the swampy conditions along its banks.

- The parking lot was relocated to its present location in 1964, and the holes were renumbered.

- The 2nd green and the 3rd tee were moved across Fuller Brook in the early 1960s.

- The sand trap in front of the 5th green was rebuilt in 1994.

- The installation of the in-ground sprinkler system was completed in 1996.

- Bigger and sturdier bridges were built across Fuller Brook on the 1st and 9th holes in the late 1990s.

- The parking lot was improved with granite curbing and plantings in 1998.

- The entrance gateway shed to the 1st tee was built in 1999.

- A single more substantial bridge replaced two bridges across Fuller Brook in 2005 to serve the 2nd and 3rd holes.

After another round at Nehoiden, Phil Connor returns to his 1966 Mustang, built a few years after the holes were renumbered and the parking lot relocated. The car was given a major restoration by his son Steve in 2003.

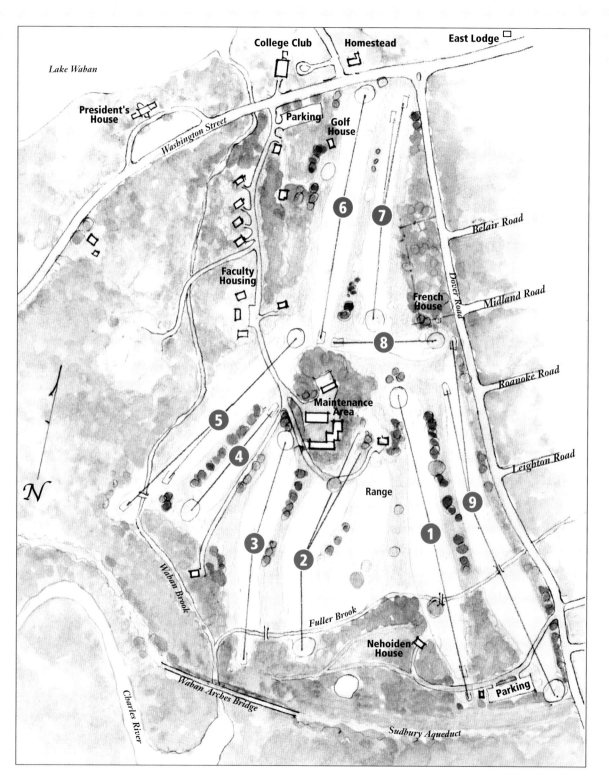

The Golf Course

Tee	Yards
Blue	3,061
White	2,931
Red	2,719

Arriving at Nehoiden

The wonderful thing about Nehoiden is its unvarnished simplicity. If you feel like playing golf, where else can you just head over to the course, put down a ball, and tee off?

Golf the way it should be! No tee times, no golf carts, usually no starter, and no fuss. And, to the consternation of some, no clubhouse. Newcomers are often puzzled by this spartan approach to the game. A number of years ago, a guest who hadn't played the course was in the parking lot looking for the clubhouse and asked where it was. "Why," Leo Madden, his host, replied with a smile, "you're standing in it."

The members don't seem to mind, and after their rounds some sit near their cars in folding chairs or use the picnic table near the 1st tee. So Madden wasn't far wrong.

But this is Nehoiden where things are often done a bit differently than they are elsewhere, their origins often lost in the mists of time.

There actually *was* a clubhouse in 1903, and it is where it's always been: adjacent to the 6th fairway, but few who play the course understand this odd historical fact. How could such a small building in the middle of a golf course—instead of near an opening or closing

hole—be the clubhouse? In 1903 the 6th was the 9th so the location made sense. Its intention was to store communal clubs so it didn't need to be large. A student publication at the time enthused about the prospect of resting "on the broad verandas of the club house" with "no more sitting down after the game in the midst of a busy community of ants"—a situation that anyone resting after their round in the utilitarian surroundings of the parking lot can easily sympathize with.

Today, as in 1900, all of the students and a few of the members who live nearby are close enough to walk to the course, but the rest drive, and a number arrive in varying degrees of style: Phil Connor in his 1966 Mustang, Ken Sullo in an immense greenish yellow 1972 Pontiac, and Hal Phillips who used to arrive in a red Honda jauntily towing his golf cart, clubs and all, behind him. David Livingston occasionally arrives in the 1931 Model A Ford Phaeton that his father bought in 1934 and that has been coming to Nehoiden ever since.

And then there is Victoria Lyo '05, captain of the College golf team, who arrives on her bicycle, golf bag slung across her shoulders, when she is playing in tournaments that begin at the 1st hole.

AT RIGHT: *Victoria Lyo '05, captain of the Wellesley College golf team, arrives at Nehoiden on her bicycle.*

FACING PAGE: *The gateway shed on the 1st tee in spring*

Things have changed since the guest asked Leo Madden where the clubhouse was. Now the parking lot features plantings, granite curbing, and a rather nice shed, built in 1999, that serves as a gateway to the 1st tee. There isn't a snack bar or even a refreshment cart, but there is a vending machine in the maintenance area and, at times, lemonade stands that are run by neighborhood children appear on the course.

In a way, Nehoiden's simplicity is reminiscent of Massachusetts' early Puritan roots and the stark 17th century divines who rode past the site on their way to examine the spiritual progress of the Native Americans, relocated to South Natick by John Eliot in 1651, and where a frequent arrival was one William Nehoiden.

The First Hole

Tee	Yards
Blue	451
White	438
Red	401

Teeing off at Nehoiden's 1st hole is a relatively informal experience. You meet up with your foursome or simply join up with a few other players already at the tee. Or you might just as likely head out alone. While things have changed at the 1st hole over the years, setting off right away has almost always been the norm at seemingly changeless Nehoiden.

The location of the 1st tee has moved four times since the course first opened in 1900. In the beginning, the hole was a 240-yard par-4, and the tee was across Fuller Brook at the beginning of the plateau on the right side of the fairway. From that point on, it played pretty much as it does today.

In the late 1920s, when a number of alterations were made to the course, a few at the suggestion of golf course architect Wayne Stiles, the hole was lengthened, and the 1st tee was moved back to what is now the portion of the parking lot nearest the 9th green. There were fewer trees then, and the hole played as a dogleg right.

In 1929, Club Secretary J. A. Symonds received permission from the Joint Committee to move the tee to the top of the Sudbury Aqueduct, which, in addition to lengthening the hole, must have made for an exciting prospect and opening drive. The tee was reached by a flight of stairs cut into the hillside to the right of the 9th green. But the delight was short-lived; in 1931, the Boston Water Company asked that the tee be moved. And so the tee finally came to rest in its present location—or locations, as there are two distinct tee boxes for the 1st hole: the back tees close to the hillside and the forward tees across the drive built in 1990.

The entrance drive runs from Dover Road across the 9th hole, between the tees on the 1st hole and then into the woods to the Arts and Crafts style Nehoiden House, built in 1990.

From 1930 through the hurricane season of 1950, golfers had more than the brook and the large oak to the left of the fairway to contend with off the 1st tee. There was a second large, though somewhat thinner, oak about 25 yards to the right of the first tree; the two oaks gave the impression that the drive was bracketed by goalposts. "Teeing off on this hole used to be like kicking an extra point," recalls longtime member Fred Nolan, who added that this second oak "was knocked over by one of the helpful hurricanes" that had ravaged the area. But this time, and only a few hours later, "the

FACING PAGE: *Town member Chris Garvin tees off from the back tee on the 1st hole.*

AT LEFT: *Nehoiden House, built in 1990, overlooks the first fairway and Fuller Brook. In 2005, it was renovated for use by the College's investment office.*

ABOVE: *The 1st green, like most of the greens at Nehoiden, is relatively small. Greenskeeper Jim Hickey planted the row of pines at the left using two and three-foot saplings that he transplanted here from elsewhere on the grounds in the mid-1970s.*

wind turned completely around and lifted the tree upright again!" However, the tree had suffered too much damage and couldn't be saved.

In 1929, the Joint Committee, presumably to help members cut their losses and speed play, voted to put chicken wire across the brook to help with golf ball retrieval. But it didn't stay in place for very long and was soon abandoned. It is not known if this system would have been of any assistance to the occasional golfer who, since 1900, has managed to fall into the brook.

The bridge over Fuller Brook has been replaced a number of times over the years, and the current incarnation is the sturdiest and broadest to date. It is so broad, in fact, that it sometimes accommodates poorly hit drives by channeling them down the fairway with a

little extra bounce and some unexpected distance. In golf, one is occasionally rewarded for doing the wrong thing. For a few years, if your ball bounded into the brook, a ball retriever thoughtfully affixed to one of the bridge's rails was there for your use.

Fuller Brook was straightened in 1958 to accommodate water-line construction and improve drainage, as its banks frequently flooded and formed a perpetual swamp.

On June 9, 1953, the 1st hole was assaulted by the most destructive tornado in New England history. It ripped through Worcester County claiming 94 lives, and its effects were felt as far away as Nehoiden. "The tornado dropped lots of debris on the course, especially on the 1st hole," recalls Fred Nolan. "The debris came all the way from Worcester and its outskirts: pieces of clothing, paper, you name it, were strewn down the fairway—so much that it was difficult to find your ball."

A prominent feature on the right side of the fairway is a handsome oak 120 yards from the green whose branches can interfere with approach shots if a ball is hit too far to the right. After this point the fairway ascends to the green and begins to narrow—partly due to the trees on the left at the top of the hill. Along with a large wire net, these trees provide a degree of protection to the clapboard house at 41 Service Drive.

This house has always been used for employee housing by Wellesley College. Nehoiden Superintendent Tony Oteri raised a family there in the 1960s and '70s. Oteri, who served for more than 33 years in the College's buildings and grounds department, remembers being rudely awakened one Sunday morning when a golf ball came through his bedroom window, bounced into the hall, then rolled down the stairs. The house and its grounds are, understandably, out of bounds.

The 1st green is quite small, as are most at Nehoiden. It is protected by a bunker to the front right and by a false front that stops approach shots dead. Just behind the green, a row of pines can stop overhit balls from disappearing down a steep hill. The recovery shot

from the bottom of this hill is daunting to say the least.

The 1st green is on the slow side. In fact, with the exception of the 9th, all of the greens register fairly low on the Stimp meter, but the members know that the high costs associated with super-fast greens would upset the wonderful balance that makes the course what it is. But then, golf has always been a game of compensating balances that are best tempered by philosophical resignation.

A tough hole? You might not think so at first, but a remarkable number of opening drives end up heading for the big oak or the brook. And the approach shot doesn't allow much room for error as it needs to hold a remarkably small green. A few of the big hitters can make it in two, but they are just as likely to take a double bogey because all parallel fairways are out of bounds, making Nehoiden that much more difficult. The 1st is ranked as Nehoiden's second toughest hole from the forward tees.

One of the nicest views at the course is back toward the tee from the 1st green. There is something pleasant about watching the golfers down below, taking their second shots—before or after the brook—and beginning their ascent.

BENCH MARK Dr. Joseph Hammer, 1907–1996

Doc Hammer (inset photo) was a Nehoiden regular who loved the course and played it often. He grew up in Boston's old West End, went to Harvard, and got his M.D. at Boston University Medical School. A lifelong general practitioner in Wellesley, he set up his practice in 1935 and retired on his 80th birthday in 1987. His office was in his home on Weston Road and his wife, Rose, was the office nurse. Doc served as a captain in the U.S. Army during World War II and treated soldiers in the South Pacific between 1944 and 1946. He is remembered as a gracious and courtly fellow with a wry smile. Many of his friends at the club were also his patients. He had a nice game and often shot in the 70s, as member Shirley Quinn recalls. He always insisted on carrying his own bag, even into his 80s. His family donated the bench shown above in his memory. Shown here, sitting on the bench, are his grandson and great-grandson, Aaron and Zachary Singer.

Richie Howard
Retired Wellesley police officer
Holes-in-One: 4th and 8th holes
Club Champion: Seven times
College Roommate: Allen Doyle, PGA
(at Norwich University)

Alice Peisch
A state representative and former town clerk, she started playing more golf when she joined in 1995. Loves ease of going out to play.
Best Shot: Chipped in on 9 after a poor round
Favorite Hole: 3 "Fewest serious obstructions"

Eddie Carens
Salesman, Golfer's Clubhouse, Natick
Best Hole: Had a double eagle (2) on the 1st hole with a 7-wood from 216 yards out
Holes-in-One: Five (none at Nehoiden)
Club Champion: 1984

The Second Hole

Most golfers who play Nehoiden for the first time usually have the same response as they approach the 2nd tee and see the massive sugar maple that overwhelms the view of the fairway: "Oh, my God!"

The prospect is a little less threatening from the forward tee. In 1900 there was another large maple of about the same size only yards farther down the fairway. This second tree disappeared some time around 1950, but since then its surviving twin has managed to get through storms and hurricanes relatively unscathed. Fred Nolan notes that "the authorities have given it a haircut a couple of times to enable a good drive to clear it." While the tree's vertical growth appears to have been arrested, its branches just get thicker and thicker each year, belying the maxim that "trees are 90 percent air." This one is about 30 percent air. Some try to hit around it. Some even try to hit under it. But basically the hole is daring you to hit a drive right over the top of it.

When the hole opened for play in 1900, it was laid out quite differently. The tee was located to the right of today's back tee in what is now thin air about 30 feet above ground level in the maintenance area. Before Nehoiden existed, this whole area was a hill that arched from the 2nd tee to the 5th green and covered nearly everything on either side.

Some time between 1928 and 1931, the tee was moved to where the forward tee sits today—either because the maintenance area was gradually expanding due to excavation of the hillside, or because the twin maples were becoming increasingly difficult to negotiate.

The fairway also changed over the years. In the early days there were no pines down its right or left sides, nor was there an out-of-bounds on the right, as the 3rd hole was in a completely different location and didn't abut the 2nd. The 2nd fairway had hazards that are long gone. Wellesley resident Ward Fearnside, who roamed the course as a lad in the 1920s, remembers that there was an old barn on the right that made teeing off much tougher, as you had to clear the twin maples while managing to avoid the barn. The 1930 score card notes a local rule no longer in force: "A ball may be lifted and dropped . . . when it is driven under the corn crib, or in, under or around the barn from No. 5 [2] tee. Penalty of one stroke." The good old days?

But perhaps worst of all, Fearnside tells of a sewer line that emptied into the end of the practice area and prompted a groundswell of interest when the nickname "Smellesley" appeared in the Boston newspapers. A short time later, the situation was remedied—probably to the

FACING PAGE: *These Japanese tree lilacs have white blossoms in early summer and provide shade for wayward balls.*

AT LEFT: *Jan Scott of the College Admissions Office tees off from the forward tee. The large sugar maple (often mistaken for an oak) on the 2nd hole becomes the primary focus of attention for golfers on both the back and forward tees.*

ABOVE: *Jack Gibson and Greg Jong observe while Scott Birney putts and Frank Mutrie holds the flag.*

The Fox and the Goose

By 1995 or 1996, Nehoiden and many other golf courses  had become the summer home for increasing numbers of Canada geese, to the point where they became a nuisance (their droppings made a mess). Many courses resorted to extreme measures such as poisoning the birds or killing them with dogs or guns. But at Nehoiden, something wonderful happened that nicely illustrates how trying too hard can often produce disastrous results. A pair of foxes built a burrow in the rough on the 2nd hole between the right side of the fairway and the brook. The built-in alarm systems of the geese started going off; they left in droves and have never returned—a morality tale in course maintenance worthy of Aesop. In 2003, several lifelike styrofoam coyotes  appeared and became successful stand-ins for these foxes.

relief of anyone with a tendency to hook.

During the 1970s and '80s, a giant lilac bush formed the point at the end of the left tree line. While the perfume that wafted from this hazard may have been sweet smelling, the lilac protruded into the fairway and snagged many a good drive. Fred Nolan reports that the bush was eventually uprooted when a College official found himself stymied by it one time too many. "He ordered it removed," Nolan recalls, "much to the satisfaction of those of us who were sometimes stuck there."

Today there is a stand of Japanese tree lilacs at the end of the row of pines on the left. The white blossoms make a pleasant canopy for the golfers whose balls have rolled under them and who will most likely need to punch a low chip back onto the fairway. The Nehoiden practice range is beyond the row of pines on the left, and it is sometimes possible to take an approach shot to the green if your ball has gone far enough in. But the practice range is out of bounds, a fact that some either choose to disregard or simply never knew.

In 1900, the hole played 247 yards to a green situated at the end of the fairway on the right. This is close to the same place used now as a temporary green when ground conditions cause the putting surface across Fuller Brook to close. Fred Nolan recalls that it was not a very difficult hole, "The green could be reached by long hitters. For years we urged the authorities to move it across the brook." As early as 1931 the members were voicing their displeasure, and the minutes of that year record their interest in making it longer.

It is not clear if any one person came up with the idea of moving the green across Fuller Brook, nor is it suggested in the Stiles plan of 1927. Some attribute the change to a bit of artistic initiative—namely, a plaster model made by Chet Brimblecom's father. Finally, in 1960, the Joint Committee decided to relocate the green to its present location beyond Fuller Brook and voted to assess the members a fee to help defray the costs of building the green as well as the 3rd tee. The assessment cost each member $40 a year for the next three years. According to Bill Donovan, superintendent from 1957

to 1962, the green was finally ready for play by mid-season 1962. As Nolan notes, "This changed the hole dramatically for the better and enhanced the overall quality of the course."

Needless to say, Fuller Brook is the recipient of many approach shots. It often happens that as you make your backswing, thoughts of the trap just behind the green intrude, and the tendency is to pull back a touch at the last instant and . . . splash. At times, small fish can be seen swimming in the water near your ball while mallards paddle on the surface. The banks of weeds in the water seem to change their positions each year, and a few balls from the driving range often end up there. Until fairly recently, there was a large oak behind the green at the left, and it would occasionally oblige by deflecting shots that were heading straight for the woods onto the surface of the green. The tree became diseased and had to be taken down in 2000.

The 2nd green is tilted upward from front to back to accept approach shots and, as there is rough between the brook and the green, hitting its surface is an all-or-nothing proposition. There are bunkers right, left, and behind. While the rough to the left isn't too bad, the area to the right is a combination of thick undergrowth, the path to the 3rd tee, and a wooded area. Woe to anyone who ends up behind the green where a bunker and an uneven strip of unforgiving hardpan make recovery difficult. If you're in the woods, the chances of getting back to the green in one are next to nil. Because the green tilts so markedly down toward the brook, even good chips from behind are hard to stop. When the course was remeasured in 2000, the 2nd was designated the number one handicap hole from the back tees.

The 2nd hole is a wonderful test of golf, and it is an exhilarating hole to par. A birdie here is truly a prized event. And bogeys are accepted gratefully. Imagine how town resident Jim Montague must have felt in the summer of 1999 when he eagled the 2nd by holing out with a seven iron from 150-yards. And he had a witness on hand who responded to his exultant exclamation, "Did you see that!" by yelling, "I did! I did!"

The Practice Facilities at Nehoiden

Situated parallel to the 2nd hole, the practice range was greatly improved in 2001 when club pro Ken Bellerose had four concrete hitting stations installed. However, many are cautioned to just use irons, otherwise their shots might rain down on players on the 2nd fairway. With flags placed at appropriate intervals and a streamside sand trap, one can get a good

Ken Bellerose giving a lesson

workout here—with everything but the driver and putter. For putting, one must go to the practice green next to the Golf House on the 6th hole.

Ken Bellerose, who arrived in 1996, gives private lessons or conducts clinics for groups, including Wellesley College employees. Ken manages to keep a tiny pro shop within the shed that backs up to 41 Service Drive, where golfers can be fitted for clubs, buy a hat or a shirt embroidered with the Nehoiden logo, or a bucket of balls for a dollar.

Balls are now retrieved with a motorized device. Until a few years ago, members had to go onto the range to pick up the balls they needed, then walk back up the hill. It recalled the days before ski lifts when skiers had to hike to the top of a hill, with skis over their shoulders, in order to ski back down.

Joy Mitchell is about to sink her putt on the practice green.

The Third Hole

HOLE

The tee for the 3rd hole backs up to the elegant Waban Arches Bridge, a large Victorian structure completed in 1876 that is part of the Sudbury Aqueduct. The bridge is a popular spot for walkers, runners, and rock climbers. Occasionally, golfers can hear the runners or climbers calling out to one another.

In 1900, the 3rd, 4th, and 5th holes were laid out in a completely different configuration, as can be seen in the site plan and explanation that appear on page 45. In the 1930s, these three "meadow holes" were redesigned. At first, the 3rd tee was moved to the left of the fairway (before it rises to form a plateau); it remained there until 1962 when the hole was lengthened by moving the tee back across Fuller Brook to its current location. "There was a swamp that extended 60 yards or so from the tee that one had to clear," recalls Fred Nolan. "Anything not airborne was lost." It was here that the term "my water hole" was frequently invoked. Ladies were not then required to hit across the swamp. Their tee was located just across it near the old incinerator on the left.

The swamp was drained when Fuller Brook was rechanneled in 1958, a move that made the 3rd "much easier from a mental hazard standpoint," according to

Nolan, and it's hard to disagree with this assessment. The new tee and brook-rerouting projects were both overseen by Superintendent Bill Donovan who, at about the same time, also planted the rows of pine trees on either side of this hole. With each passing year they have further defined the fairway.

While the 3rd is probably the simplest par-4 on the course, the golfer does need to get across Fuller Brook successfully. Even though it runs quietly along no more than ten yards from the end of the tee box, the evidence suggests that not all are successful in getting across—its banks are excellent places to find golf balls.

The drive requires accuracy since going too far to the right brings the pines and out-of-bounds into play, and this error often makes for a difficult second shot.

The approach shot also requires a degree of caution because the 3rd green is protected by bunkers to the front left and to the right. And it isn't a good idea to overshoot the green as Service Drive, a few yards beyond, is out of bounds. Until the 1970s, there had also been a bunker to the left of the green; its outline, in heavy rough, can still be seen.

The putting surface here is basically flat and, all in

FACING PAGE: *The marker bush for the 2nd fairway, at right, is no longer accurate for the 2nd hole but has become useful for the 3rd where it can serve as a measurement guide: it is 132 yards from this bush to the center of the 3rd green.*

AT LEFT: *Having completed the 2nd hole, some golfers wend their way through the woods to the 3rd tee.*

all, the hole is not especially challenging. But scoring a birdie or par is not done all that frequently, so the hole often becomes a true test of the golfer's equanimity after carding, say, a double bogey. Eddie Carens admittedly felt chagrined when he scored a double bogey here in 2003 after birdying the 2nd and getting a double-eagle two (yes, a two!) on the 1st hole, a par-5.

During the fall of 2002, several surveyors measured the area between the 2nd green and the 3rd tee.

When they had finished, little ribbons appeared on a number of trees in preparation for another bridge building project that began during early 2005. The area had been served by two wooden bridges ever since the 1960s. The wider and more substantial new bridge serves both holes—it is a bit closer to the 3rd tee due to a sewer line in this section of the course. And state conservation commission guidelines have resulted in a few new wrinkles in the approach to the 2nd green.

The Meadow Holes

The early golf courses in New England were relatively short, but eventually most set about remedying this situation. The 2,100-yard Nehoiden course was lengthened between 1928 and 1932, and the 6th, 7th, and 8th "meadow holes" of 1900 shown at right were completely reorganized and ultimately became today's 3rd, 4th, and 5th. In 1900, the land between the practice fairway and Waban Brook was one big meadow. The plan at right shows how the old 6th lay perpendicular to today's 3rd; the old 7th went in the opposite direction of today's 4th; and the 8th (replaced by today's 5th) was a short par-3 to the top of a hill that no longer exists due to the excavations for the maintenance area.

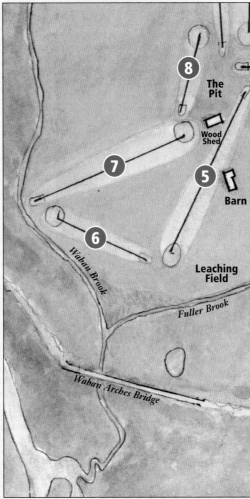

ABOVE: *Today the redesigned meadow holes have been separated by pine trees. Tim Hoey, custodial manager at Wellesley College, tees off.*

TOP RIGHT: *A golfer stands on what seems to be the old 7th (more or less today's 4th) with open space and the Waban Arches Bridge in the background.*

Kathy Schleyer

An administrator at the Wellesley Centers for Women, she learned to play golf in Manhattan. She golfed at Clearview in Queens and got there by subway, clubs and all—she points out that in New York City no one is especially conspicuous.
Best Shots: Once one-putted all nine greens in the rain.
Favorite Hole: The 6th "It's the most exciting."

Elisa Romano and Nick and Mike Blair

Elisa Romano, M.D. often plays with her sons, both of whom picked up clubs when they were 6. Elisa has been playing since she was 16 and was on the UMass team in college. During the summers she worked at Crumpin Fox selling golf balls and gin and tonics. Nick made the high school team as a freshman in 2003. Mike and Elisa tied for first place in the 2003 MGA Mother-Son Tournament.

Mike Dowling

WCVB-TV sportscaster and reporter, he emceed the dinner celebrating the MGA's 100th in 2003 at The Copley Plaza. Loves being able to play Nehoiden anytime, usually with his sons, in a casual, friendly atmosphere.
Favorite Approach: On the 6th "It's fun when you finally get a view of the green and see if your shot is as good as you thought it was."

The Fourth Hole

Originally the 4th hole played in the opposite direction. Its tee was close to the forward tee on the 5th and the fairway came straight back up the existing tree line between the 4th and 5th holes. It wasn't until 1929 that the hole was rerouted, along with the other meadow holes, and reversed its direction. At first, the tee was much further back, on the other side of Service Drive and close to the stockade fence that now prevents approach shots to the 5th green from going into the western edge of the maintenance area.

In the photograph on page 49, it is easy to visualize the former tee near the stockade fence and, in the foreground of this photograph, the lighter grass indicates where the green was once located. At that time, the 4th played as a 227-yard par-4. However, there were problems. Golfers on the 4th tee were exposed to errant shots intended for the 5th green, and players around the 3rd green were too close to tee shots from the 4th. In early 1950, the Joint Committee, citing safety concerns, moved the 4th tee and green to their current locations, thereby creating a very solid 200-yard par-3.

There is no doubt that this is a tough hole. A straight tee shot is required for par as there is trouble all along the right with the row of pines that routinely knocks balls down. Along the left, a narrow paved road runs the full length of the hole leading to what used to be an incinerator site. Anything left of this road is out of bounds, although it usually takes a while before most newcomers to the course realize this unfortunate fact of Nehoiden life.

The bunkers around the hole regularly catch balls that travel just a bit too much to the right or the left.

And should you strike the ball a bit too forcefully, it can go behind the green and down a hill where it may come to a halt at a recently installed chain link fence. The good news is that without the fence your ball could have jumped into a swamp, and there would have been little chance of ever finding it; the bad news is that you now have an exceptionally difficult recovery shot, as your lie is probably not very good and there are overhanging branches to contend with as you try to gently loft the ball back up to the green.

It's not clear how many green-side bunkers were built in concert with this 1933 green, or how many were left over from the original green. This much we do know: the green that survives to this day can be exacting, with a ridge extending in from the left bunker.

As he had elsewhere on the course, Nehoiden Superintendent Bill Donovan planted the line of pine trees which has grown into a mature barrier down the right side of the fairway.

FACING PAGE: *Member Barbara Hernberg tees off.*

AT LEFT: *While space dictates the spelling, the sign on the basket is phonetically correct (in this state).*

The 3rd and 4th offer a degree of relief as the green and tee are adjacent to the maintenance area. In 1968, the Joint Committee voted to install restrooms there and, in 2002, a computer terminal was added for maintaining handicaps. The maintenance area garages house the equipment used to maintain the course and the College grounds and a lost-and-found barrel for the golfers. The area between the 3rd green and the 4th tee also contains the club's tournament and announcement bulletin boards. In recent years the tee has been enhanced with a variety of plantings.

From time to time, the grounds crew sets out a basket at the 4th tee that is filled with balls found on the course. They can be purchased at a very reasonable rate, though members are occasionally challenged by the honor system when recognizing any of their lost balls.

FACING PAGE: *The 4th green with the sprinklers in action*
ABOVE: *In 1930, the tee (point A) was across Service Drive and the green (point B) was in the area of the lighter-colored grass in the foreground.*

BENCH MARK   Charlie Gubellini, 1913–1997

Charlie Gubellini grew up in Wellesley and was a football and track star at the high school. He won a football scholarship to Boston University and played four years on the varsity team. At the outset of World War II, he enlisted in the U.S. Army and, being fluent in French and Italian, was assigned to Counterintelligence. Two days after D-Day he landed at Omaha Beach, spent time in France, and then became agent-in-charge in Brussels. Charlie won the Bronze Star for capturing Paul Alisch, the second most-wanted spy in the Third Reich. In his capacity as a priest, Alisch would hear confessions of French Resistance fighters and then report them to the Gestapo. Charlie (in uniform in the inset photo) worked closely with Inspector Van Horick (at left) of the Belgian Sûreté. After the war he was head coach of the Wellesley High School football team and led the Raiders to their first untied, unbeaten season in 1952. Charlie was an architectural representative for several lumber companies including US Plywood, where he was employed for 27 years. He was president of the Nehoiden Men's Group and also served as handicap chairman. He and his wife, Marian (longtime chair of the women's handicap committee), built a home in the Woodlands section of Wellesley in 1955. Seated on his bench—donated by the Men's Group and the Gubellini Family—is Charlie's son Peter, also a Nehoiden golfer.

Charles "Mickey" Walsh
Fitness and health teacher teacher in the Wellesley elementary school system, he lives in West Roxbury and likes Nehoiden's low-key and unpretentious atmosphere.
Best Shot: 8" from cup on the 8th
Favorite Hole: The 9th "It's an honest par 5."

Catherine Feddersen '84
Alumnae co-chair of Friends of Wellesley College Athletics, she played lacrosse and swam in college. Started playing golf in '85 but not regularly until joining NWGA in 2000. Won Dell Murphy Cup for Most Improved Player in 2003.
Favorite Hole: The 8th "Best chance for par"

Jack Gibson
A retired abrasives salesman, he joined in 1981.
Best Shot: Chipped out of the trap at the top of the hill on the 6th hole and then watched the ball roll right into the cup. Plays Nehoiden just about every day.
Favorite Hole: The 7th

The Fifth Hole

The view from the back tee on the 5th hole is one of Nehoiden's most attractive, with pines framing the right side and a large oak guarding the elevated green. Well beyond the green is a row of pines and, above them, an impressive expanse of sky. Whether or not the golfer is inspired by the view, it is imperative that the ball go at least beyond Waban Brook in front of the back tees.

Originally the 5th hole was a short uphill par-3 with the tee sited somewhere near today's 4th tee. The green was to the right of today's 5th green, probably in what is now just air but which was then a part of the hillside that was ultimately excavated to accommodate the maintenance area. The old hole was never popular because there was a good deal of heavy rough and undergrowth between tee and green.

In the 1930s, when serious change was afoot and the meadow holes were completely redone and rerouted, the little uphill 5th was combined with the 4th and moved closer to Waban Brook. Later, the back tees were pushed across the brook.

Waban Brook, which runs from Lake Waban to the Charles River, had originally run much further to the west but was rerouted to drain what is now a College biodegradable dump site and to form the left side of the hole. The brook is now a lateral hazard that frequently floods the fairway during heavy rains. Fish were seen swimming in the fairway in 1998. The flooding is an occasional inconvenience, and the often soggy fairway conditions deaden ball roll and make the hole play longer. And, when the fairway is flooded, most golfers, from the back tees, need to give serious consideration to laying up.

The ideal drive on 5 is down the right where the fairway is less likely to be soggy and the ball will have greater roll. This puts the ball on the side of the fairway where it has the best chance of getting beyond the pronounced ridge formed by a pipeline, which angles across the entire fairway, and is the best approach to the green. The approach shot needs to be especially accurate. Balls that go too far to the right make recovery from the area below the steep bank to the green highly problematic. The best plan

FACING PAGE: *The view from the back tee is impressive, but the golfer needs, first and foremost, to get the ball across Waban Brook and out beyond the forward tee.*

AT LEFT: *Shannon Hartmann and Joan Gorman putt out. Holding the 5th green is often a problem as its surface slopes gently down from front to back. Approach shots that seem perfect often end up on the back fringe or worse.*

Nehoiden's Wild Mushrooms . . . or Cosmic Humor

The question has been asked: "Why, of all the things that might be growing on a golf course, would they be white, round, and pretty much the size of golf balls?" A satisfactory answer has yet to be found. While these photos of *Agaricus campestris* were taken on the hill going up to the 5th green, this mushroom can be found on most of Nehoiden's holes when the conditions are right. If mushroom remains are anything to judge by, it would seem that some golfers vent their irritation by swinging at them with a club.

From 20 yards:
"There's my ball!"

From 10 yards:
"Is that a ball?"

From 5 yards:
"Accchh! It's a mushroom!"

Kimberly Goff-Crews
Wellesley's dean of students lives in the faculty house that overlooks the 5th green. While a nongolfer as of this writing, she has plans to take up the game in the near future.
She grew up in Los Angeles.

FACING PAGE: *Nehoiden member Harold Becker attempts to blast out of the bunker beneath the green.*

when stuck in this area is to chip back to the fairway, but most try to pop the ball up and fly it to the green, though not all succeed.

Service Drive crosses the hole at the foot of the steep hill beneath the green and occasionally provides a huge assist to approach shots that hit its surface and literally vault up to, or near, the green. For faculty golfers who live on Service Drive, the 5th is usually the last in their round.

On the left of the steep hill below the green there was once an exceptionally large bunker that has been called many names, though "Big Sahara" is probably the nicest. It was, by any standard, a daunting hazard and was literally as wide as the green. It was also deep—occupying the entire hillside on which the green is perched—and prevented anyone standing in it from seeing the flag (even if the pin were located five paces from the front edge). It was a magnet and gathered in all manner of ill-executed approach shots with alarming regularity. However, the location and size of the bunker threatened the entire hillside and green with erosion. In the mid-1990s, the club was obliged to act to save the 5th green. Today we are left with the smaller heart-shaped bunker—still a difficult hazard, but one with about half of its predecessor's torments.

The 5th green has one of Nehoiden's most dramatically sited putting surfaces. As one crests the hill, the view of this green—bounded by steep banks back and left, an overhanging oak, and the bunker guarding the front—is only enhanced by the anticipation of where one's ball might have come to rest. Too often, it has run to the rear fringe as the green subtly tilts down from front to back. The entire putting surface appears quite level but for some reason remains difficult to read, and its surroundings hint at breaks that simply aren't there.

For many years since the 1930s, the 5th hole was rated as the number one handicap hole on the course from the back tees, but recent remeasuring and the official MGA rating in 2002 dropped it into third place after the 2nd and 9th holes. Nevertheless, the 5th is still a demanding hole as there is trouble right and left, and the trap is a major forward hazard. Yet, there is trouble right, left, fore, and aft on the number one 2nd hole, and the brook poses easily as much a psychological threat as the big bunker on the 5th. But lest there be any doubt, the 5th is still a tough hole to par.

In 2003, member Tom Kelley was playing in a Saturday morning round with Brian Walmsley and hit his approach shot right at the flag. When they got to the green and didn't see a second ball, they began searching the hillside at the back of the green. But nothing was to be found. Brian walked past the cup to his ball, and he looked in. There it was. Tom had eagled the hole! It was something that Nehoiden membership coordinator Jim Donahue reports has either never happened before or, indeed if it has, it must have been beyond living memory.

The Flora of the Fifth

While the golf course has become more and more colorful in recent years thanks to the plantings that have been made by the grounds crew, Nehoiden offers its own flora that make a round of golf that much more pleasant, though in the case of the omnipresent mushroom, *Agaricus campestris*, that much more confounding. Many golfers have been charmed by the blackberries and wild roses (*Rosa blanda*) that grow along the banks of Waban Brook. Some golfers make a point of walking along the left side of the fairway during blackberry season in order to pick some of the berries and eat them—a pleasant diversion to their round.

Marilyn and Travis Nutting

Marilyn taught art for many years in the Wellesley elementary schools and now works part time at the town library. Travis was with Paine Webber in Boston in institutional trading. Hardly a day goes by that the Nuttings don't get in nine holes at Nehoiden. Travis is a past president of the Men's Group and has won both the Men's Group Class B and Class C championships, and Marilyn has been active in the Women's Group.

The Sixth Hole

Tee	Yards
Blue	369
White	355
Red	350

There are many reasons why the 6th is the best candidate for Nehoiden's signature hole, and not just because it offers one of the most startlingly blind greens in New England. It's the hole where the College students and the town members regularly come in close contact because of the classes held on the 6th fairway, and it's from the 6th that players get their best view of the College's magnificent Galen Stone Tower. It's also where we have our closest connection to the Native Americans who lived in the region; arrowheads were discovered in the vicinity of the practice putting green in the 1920s. The 6th is also the closest point on the course to the spot on Waban Brook where John Eliot built a sawmill for the Native Americans in 1651 and where Nehoiden himself was a frequent visitor. The 6th green is across the street from Homestead, the house where the founders of Wellesley College first lived while accumulating the estate that they began turning into a college in 1870. And lastly, while few in the outside world are familiar with Nehoiden, just about everyone who has traveled along Route 16 is familiar with the 6th green—they usually don't know the name of the course, but they do know the green. From time to time some of these passersby remind us of their presence by honking their horns if someone sinks a putt, or they demonstrate their remarkably uniform sense of humor by yelling, "Fore!"

The College has long conducted its golf classes, offered through the Physical Education, Recreation, and Athletics Department, on the 6th and 7th holes. If the orange flag is flying on the Golf House, golf classes have convened—the 6th and 7th are off limits. At these times, players proceed directly to the conveniently adjoining 8th tee.

It's a happy quirk of Nehoiden's routing that allows this seamless exclusion of 6 and 7, an option many employ even when class isn't in session if the golfers A) are beginning to tire and/or prefer to eliminate the steep climb to the 7th tee, B) are running late and must cut the round short, or perhaps C) are stuck behind a slow group that won't let them through (in defiance of the courtesy the game requires). They may seize this opportunity to pass—provided the group playing the 7th isn't inconvenienced. This routing option and the off-chance that the College students are in class mean that the 6th and 7th are undoubtedly the most frequently skipped holes at Nehoiden.

When the 6th hole is open for play, driving to a playable spot in its crumpled, uneven fairway isn't exactly a given, what with thick brush, pine woods, and out-of-bounds stakes to the left or, to the right, the out-of-bounds 7th fairway. But the 6th fairway is quite generous, and driving the ball here is merely a prelude to the hole's most obvious challenge, namely, the blind approach to a green sitting between an especially annoying, ball-accumulating ledge and a spot no more than five yards

CAUTION
PLEASE BE AWARE
PUBLIC ROADS & WALKWAYS ARE
LOCATED AT BOTTOM OF GREEN

FACING PAGE: *Mark Rothwell, son of groundsman Bernie Rothwell, prepares to tee off on a perfect October afternoon.*

AT LEFT: *A warning sign of things to come*

BENCH MARK   Willie Furdon, 1952–1995

Willie Furdon was born and raised in Wellesley. He went to the Fiske School and the junior high and, after graduating from high school, went to work for the Wellesley highway department. As a boy, he caddied for his father, Bill, at Nehoiden and soon learned to play golf. He was one of many town employees to spend happy days out on the course. His mother Gertrude, father Bill, and sister Barbara are shown sitting on his bench which is directly behind the 6th tee.

HISTORICAL MARKER
Native American Camp Site

In the early 1920s, many arrowheads and flints were discovered between the practice green and Golf House by ball hawk Ward Fearnside and his brother. The arrowheads could have been made at any time between 5000 BC and 1651 AD by Native Americans camping on the 6th fairway. The site, with its access to Waban Brook and fresh water, was ideal for a campground. The arrowhead at left was found in Natick and is from the Woodland Period (3000 to 2500 BC). It is on display at the Natick Historical Society Museum in the Bacon Library.

from the unforgiving pavement of Washington Street. Until 1957 there was another challenging hazard on this hole: a huge elm that stood less than ten yards from the putting surface. The ledge where this tree was situated in the hillside is still plainly evident today.

To any passing pedestrian or motorist, the elm tree would have offered a degree of protection from overhit balls. To the Nehoiden golfer, it was a devil in barked clothing. For more than half a century, until the sprawling giant finally keeled over during a storm in 1957, this elm was the most menacing tree on a golf course replete with enormous, improbably placed trees. "There was a little window of opportunity to the right of the tree," Fred Nolan explains, "but the best strategy involved a low shot that rolled down the hill, under its overhanging branches. The more adventurous players lofted shots right into the branches where the ball would bounce around and once in a while drop near the hole."

One of the most amusing things about accompanying a first-time player at Nehoiden is the inevitable explanation of just how to approach the 6th green. It goes something like this: "See the telephone pole above the roof of that house straight ahead? See the gooseneck street lamp to its right? Well, the green is between them, and the hill is bowl-shaped. Take one club less and hit toward the gooseneck lamp as it plays pretty much straight down hill, and the bowl will pull it left."

Explaining this to the Nehoiden newcomer, members cannot help but feel a sense of affection for their unconventional club and its peculiar 6th hole—"Just hit it and hope." That the 6th green is also one of the smallest on the course only enhances its singular challenge, for veterans and first-timers alike.

Most golf courses don't offer holes that come any blinder than the 6th at Nehoiden. Approach shots float or bound over the horizon and simply disappear; there's little telling where they might end up. If there's any wind, all bets are off. Well-aimed approaches are as likely to hang up on the hill as they are to fly the green entirely. And there's nothing quite so demoralizing as watching a well-played approach shot vanish over the horizon, only to see it bounce back up into view off the street below.

Flying one's approach shot onto the 6th green is a daring but common strategy today; balls hit and stop if the distance is right. But harking back to when the elm was still standing, we can see that a hold-over strategy remains perfectly effective: low, running shots played down the hill would have avoided the big elm, and today they continue to reduce the odds of airmailing the ball onto the road and out of bounds.

The only deterrent to this throwback tactic is a sizable cross-bunker which sits at the hill's crest beside a large swale. They are not deterrents to everyone, this bunker and swale. Most tee shots can't reach them, and some approach shots sail right over them. Even a well-played bump-and-run approach can land on the downhill, well beyond the bunker. For most, however, these hazards pose a very real challenge—gobbling up both tentative approach shots and lay-ups played too boldly.

Aerial photographs of the course from the 1930s show no evidence of this bunker. When and why it was built is not clear. Wayne Stiles' 1927 plan called for moving the 6th green up the hill, well away from the street. Clearly this portion of his plan was never implemented. It's possible this bunker was built to protect a prototype green, as a test of Stiles' idea, or maybe to bound a temporary green when Route 16 was widened in 1964. Or perhaps the bunker was installed after the elm came down in 1957, purposely adding difficulty to a hole that had just become much easier. Whatever its genesis, the bunker survives, equal parts ornament and hazard.

Nehoiden regulars have developed the practical habit of leaving their bags near the 7th tee before descending to the 6th green, and toting only those clubs necessary to hole out.

The number of times one has played the 6th hole doesn't diminish the sense of anticipation as the green comes into view. Where is my ball? Is that yours on the green, or is it mine? What felt like a perfect approach could be in the street or on the hill, or nestled beside the split rail fence that separates golf course from sidewalk. There is just no telling.

AT RIGHT: *Proof positive that there really was a large elm that blocked the approach to the 6th green until 1957.*

Joh Kokubo
Wellesley College Club executive chef, he attended the French Culinary Institute in New York City and began golfing at Nehoiden in 2001.
Favorite Hole: The 6th ("A chip from where I work.")
Wildest Shot: Hit the tree on 8, rolled just past the cup. Missed the putt. Took par. Was thankful.

Victoria Lyo '05
She is a chemistry and biology double major.
Home Town: San Francisco
Golf Team Captain: 2003 to 2005
Team Member: '01–'05 **Handicap:** 12
Best Hole: Birdie on 2 (after a 3' putt)
Plans after Graduation: Medical school

Phil Grupposo
President of the Independent Maintenance and Service Employees Union of America at the College and lead custodian. Member, Nehoiden Men's Group.
Best Round: 78 (38/40) Stresses this is not the norm.
Eagle: 3rd hole (with driver and 7 iron)
Favorite Hole: The 6th

Stacey Eady '06
A member of the golf team, she is interested in a career in environmental law.
Home Town: Boulder, Colorado
Favorite Hole: The 6th—she gets a kick out of the possibility that someone will actually hit Homestead with an approach shot.

The Seventh Hole

Tee	Yards
Blue	309
White	297
Red	296

It was partly due to the neighbors on Dover Road across from the 7th tee that the renumbering of Nehoiden's holes took place in 1964. In 1900, the 7th was the opening hole, which made a lot of sense because it was right across the street from the campus. But because the course had always had town members, parking became a problem when the membership grew. It was exacerbated when the Wellesley College Club was built in 1963. This problem was finally solved with a simple solution: the 4th hole became the 1st, and a new parking lot was built well away from any of the neighbors.

It's safe to say that no hole at Nehoiden—in terms of yardage, routing, and overall integrity— has been the object of less tinkering than this 309-yard par-4. Today's 7th hole plays very much as it did in 1900, and whether you play the blue, white, or red tees, you are faced

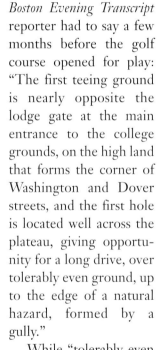

pretty much with the same distance and challenges.

In 1900, the 7th hole was the 1st. Here's what *The Boston Evening Transcript* reporter had to say a few months before the golf course opened for play: "The first teeing ground is nearly opposite the lodge gate at the main entrance to the college grounds, on the high land that forms the corner of Washington and Dover streets, and the first hole is located well across the plateau, giving opportunity for a long drive, over tolerably even ground, up to the edge of a natural hazard, formed by a gully."

While "tolerably even ground" remains a fair assessment of the fairway, there is an oval-shaped, flat-bottomed depression that extends into the plateau some 150 yards from the tee. Unless the ball comes to rest on one of its inclines, the depression doesn't pose much of a hazard. Inside it, stances are level and views of the

FACING PAGE: *The 7th green absorbs the light on a fall evening as dusk approaches. Golfers are putting out on the 8th green, and the 9th tee is ready and waiting for them.*

AT LEFT: *Framingham High School English teacher and Wellesley College teaching associate Will Cook tees off.*

BENCH MARK Irene Goddard, 1912–1995

Irene Goddard was born and raised in Upper Graniteville, Vermont, an area noted for its extensive granite quarries. She went to Spaulding High School in Barre where she was an all-district basketball player. It wasn't until after she had graduated from high school that she developed her two lifelong avocations: golf and skiing. She moved to Wellesley in 1940 when she married J. Holmes Goddard, Jr., then moved away in 1943 when her husband was transferred to the midwest. They returned in the early 1960s, and Irene worked at the College for 10 years in a variety of positions and played golf at Nehoiden until 1985. Shown above is Irene in her earlier years on the links, and seated on her bench is her son Brooks Goddard, known to many in town as the popular head of the Wellesley High School English Department, although he is now retired.

green are not obscured. As it does on so many holes at Nehoiden, trouble at the 7th begins when one doesn't find the fairway.

The parallel 6th hole, to the right, is out of bounds, but if a player misses left, the obstacles are more varied. The wooded area left of the fairway has always been rife with underbrush.

Don Crawshaw remembers an especially nasty ball-eating bush that used to be located about 150 yards down the left side. It consisted of a low, impenetrable clump of Scotch pines and was the resting place of many a duck hook. Crawshaw recalls that "about 150 balls were found when it was removed in the early 1990s." More recently, member Jack Beggs reports that a cousin of this Scotch pine, the old 150-yard cedar marker bush, is also the repository of unfortunate drives. If you check it out carefully, you will often find a ball or two wedged in its tightly knit branches. This marker bush is one of the few still remaining that members Don Gardner and Pat Murphy purchased and planted in 1958.

Today, hooked drives are more likely to encounter the fence that defines the property boundary of 29 Dover Road. This wooden enclosure begins in the deep rough and extends perpendicular to the fairway, before turning left at a 90-degree angle. It has stymied countless shots over the years. From its pockmarked facade, we could argue that golfers have doled out their own measure of punishment. Pulls and hooks which clear the fence are out of bounds too, and a bit of discreet signage warns golfers that balls hit into the backyard at 29 Dover are duly "lost" and are not to be retrieved. The fence hasn't always been there, of course. The house was built in the 1920s, and the barrier came sometime afterward, most likely during the 1950s. Even so, the large pines in the backyard of 29 Dover Road, which today hang over the fence, tell us that left of the 7th fairway has never been an easy place from which to recover. In recent years, some of the

undergrowth has been cleared out, making it somewhat easier to find your ball if mishaps occur.

Should one hit a long drive down the left side that lands on the perennially dry hardpan by the fence, driving distance is significantly increased by the roll.

From the fairway, the trap just left of the green would appear to guard the putting surface. But this is an illusion, as it actually sits some 25 yards short of the green—and the deception actually works in the golfer's favor. It subtly warns players about missing the green left, where a gully and a large oak patiently wait. Chipping up to the green from the gully is a chancy affair.

The bunker right of the green closely hugs the putting surface, swallowing up any approach shots that might drift its way. The semicircular bunker that rings the back side of the green is one of Nehoiden's hidden hazards. It's also curious, as it doesn't flank the green at all closely and rarely comes into play. Yet careful study of Nehoiden's old plans explains this bunker's peculiar placement. The original putting surface here was located much closer to the edge of the gully. This meant the putting surface bordered this semicircular bunker quite closely and was a friendly hazard because it caught strong approaches that might otherwise have plunged over the green, or left of it and into the deep gully.

The 7th is for many a deceptive hole. Its wide straight fairway with no obvious impediments invites thoughts of an easy par. Players are often fooled by the illusion that the approach shot to the green is closer than it really is and that the green is flatter than is actually the case. It not only tips to the back but has subtle curves and undulations that can easily be misread.

Wayne Stiles' plan shows he had a particularly grand concept in mind for the 7th hole in 1927. He proposed that the current green be scrapped and that the hole play across to what is today's 1st green. This would have turned the 7th into a par-4 measuring 410 yards, and unquestionably it would have become a very demanding hole.

Judy C. Brown
Professor of physics at Wellesley College
and 2003 Nine-Hole Women's Champion. Having been
attracted to the game from afar while growing up in Texas, Judy
finally took up golf in 1992. She has been at the College
since the 1960s.

Jean and Al Gismondi
These Wellesley residents joined in 1994. Jean is in finance and Al
has a graphic design firm. They frequently play together and have taken
lessons with Nehoiden pro Ken Bellerose. Al's favorite hole is 2, which he
has birdied and parred, and Jean's is 6, although her best shots
have been when she reached the green on the 2nd in two.
They both love the fact that tee times aren't required.
Al has a design firm, and Jean is in finance with IBM in Cambridge.

Sabreen Aziz Baig '07
She has taken golf classes and wants to
play as much as she can while at Wellesley.
From: Lahore, Pakistan
Major: Mathematics and economics
She plans to return to Pakistan to work in these fields.

Golf-Ball Recycling Facility

Despite the fact that a large net has been placed on the left and a stockade fence installed to deflect golf balls, a great many golf balls still end up in the backyard of 29 Dover Road. Ben Berg is a resident of this embattled home, and he made pocket money by selling at the standard Nehoiden rate of four balls for a dollar, although, on the advice of one of the members, he upped the price to a dollar apiece for Titleist Pro V1s. Robert Berg, Ben's father and a professor of physics at the College, is a Nehoiden member and admits to having a grasp on the physics of the golf swing but not, as yet, its execution.

HISTORICAL MARKER   Bullard's Tavern

On April 19, 1775, the news that the British had landed was brought by horseback to Ephraim Bullard's tavern. When Bullard heard the news, he ran to the top of a nearby hill and fired his gun three times, the signal for the West Needham Minutemen to rally. Across Washington Street near East Lodge, about 200 yards from the 7th tee, a marker commemorates the site of the tavern where the 42 Minutemen gathered. They met up with two other West Needham units and saw action when they attacked the retreating British forces in the Arlington area. Several Bullards, Fullers, and a Dewing were in the combined Needham force which lost six men. The memorial shown here replaced one that Pauline Durant dedicated in 1911.

The Eighth Hole

Today's 8th may look like a triumph of canny, lay-of-the-land design, but nothing on this 148-yard hole is original. Just about everything was fashioned by human hands. From the club's opening in 1900 to the early 1930s, the 8th was a very different hole from what we know today.

As seen in the 1900 layout (on page 7), the original green was farther down Dover Road, opposite the foot of Roanoke Road. And the original tee was about 25 yards to the right of its current location, on the elevated land that existed before the maintenance area was carved out of the hillside.

Visualizing how all this looked *circa* 1900 requires some imagination. The promontory of land that today accommodates the 6th and 8th tees, the 2nd tee, the 1st green, and the 9th tee, was all of one piece. Furthermore, in the days before Service Drive, access to the house between the 1st green and 2nd tee was provided by an entrance drive that was an extension of Midland Road.

Over time, College excavators scraped away at the promontory, eventually creating two separate hills with the maintenance area in between. The access road was now on an embankment that stretched from the back corner of the French House property to the hill behind the 1st green; it was high enough to require an especially long pin for the green (see the 1935 course layout on page 17). The area from the 8th tee to the far side of the embankment was very heavy rough, and players had to carry this elevated road to reach the green. After the houses on Service Drive were built, this road was extended to the house by the 2nd tee, and shortly afterward, the Midland Road entrance was closed, the embankment eliminated, and the 8th hole became what we know today.

While the 8th hole is Nehoiden's shortest, it is by no means a foregone conclusion that reaching the green is a simple accomplishment. The golfer must hit a shot that's long enough to clear the bunker in front and straight enough to avoid the bunker to the right, or the tree-bunker combination to the left. And if a ball is hit too far it can end up on the 9th tee, which makes chipping back a tough proposition. Once on the green, however, putting is not an easy matter as the

FACING PAGE: *A threesome heads to the 8th green.*

AT LEFT: *French House—or 33 Dover Road—was built in the Arts and Crafts style. It was a private home until it was acquired by the College in 1960 and is now used as a small dormitory where French is spoken exclusively.*

green slopes down precipitously from back to front and has curves and undulations that make it even more interesting.

Nonetheless, the 8th is where most of Nehoiden's holes-in-one do occur, so it is fitting that the bench at the back of the tee is dedicated to Donny Allen, who had a hole-in-one here on September 1, 1984, a feat he was always very proud of.

Among those who have had the thrill of getting a hole-in-one on the 8th is Women's Group member Lee Potter. And then there are Jim Donahue and Dick Nickeson, who have both done it twice! A good many others, too numerous to name, have also aced the 8th, and many more have come very close.

FACING PAGE: *The 8th green slopes down from the 9th tee. Facing the camera is Steve Rabin, a Nehoiden regular.*

ABOVE: *One of the three sand traps that protect the green*

BENCH MARK
Donald J. Allen, 1939–1989

Donny Allen (inset) was born in Somerville and raised in Wayland. In 1961, after returning from Germany, where he served in the U.S. Army, he joined the Wellesley Municipal Light Plant as a lineman and worked there for the next 28 years. Allen was an avid golfer and was very proud of his hole-in-one on the 8th hole. Pictured on his bench are his grandson Donald Allen III, his daughter-in-law Debbie, his son Donald Allen, Jr., and his granddaughter Melissa. Allen was very popular among town employees, and in 1989 his friends and fellow Nehoiden golfers named a tournament for him. A few years later, they combined his name with Willie Furdon's, another golfer and town employee who had also died (see Bench Mark on the 6th). Now known as the Memorial Tournament, it is also in memory of town employee Michael Scott. Joe Marenghi, who retired from the Light Plant and is now on the Nehoiden grounds crew, learned to play golf at Nehoiden at Allen's urging. Joe remembers him as warmhearted, outgoing, and very enthusiastic about the game and Nehoiden. The Memorial Tournament is played in the fall, and the tournament plaques are displayed in the Light Plant offices.

Peter Bracken
A line supervisor with the Wellesley Municipal Light Plant, he has been a member since the mid-1980s. He learned to play at Nehoiden with Donny Allen's encouragement and tries to play once a week.
Hole-in-One: 4th hole with a 3-iron from 200 yards

Lee Potter
Took up golf around 1989
Hole-in-One: 8th hole
Represents the NWGA in the Spring League of the Massachusetts Women's Golf Association.
Favorite Hole: 6th "The most interesting. It's fun to see where your approach shot lands."
Favorite Season: "Fall—it's so beautiful and there are very few players on the course."

Dick Nickeson
A member since 1983, he is a retired sales manager, plays many golf courses, and greatly enjoys the pickup rounds he has at Nehoiden. **Best Round:** 35/38
Hole-in-One: 8th hole (twice)
Had a 2" putt for eagle on the 1st, struck the ball too firmly, and had to settle for a birdie.

The Ninth Hole

Tee	Yards
Blue	531
White	508
Red	464

Nehoiden's magnificent 9th—the layout's longest and, some would argue, most demanding hole—didn't start out as a par-5. Originally it was barely a par-4 with everyone using today's forward tee and the green on the near side of the brook. During the late 1920s, when Nehoiden underwent so much change, this hole was lengthened by extending it well beyond Fuller Brook and creating today's back tee which was expanded in 1970.

In 1900, Dover Road formed a deterrent on the left, but many of the trees which separate the 1st and 9th holes weren't even in existence. Under the direction of Bill Donovan, the sprawling Fuller Brook was channeled into its present course in the late 1950s—as part of an effort to curb the frequent flooding problems that had greatly increased in the wake of two especially bad hurricanes, Carol and Diane. Until Fuller Brook was channeled and straightened, the approach to the green was much tougher. The brook formed a swampy lagoon that had to be carried, and there was yet another mighty tree on the right side of the fairway near the brook. Until a storm felled it during the 1950s, this enormous tree further complicated fairway shots on the 9th.

In the 1940s, "A good drive to anywhere from the center to the right side of the fairway stymied the player, in that a lofted iron was required to clear the tree and the brook beyond it," recalls Fred Nolan. "That done, the player still needed a long third shot to reach the green. Longer hitters who avoided the tree could hit a fairway wood to about where the driveway entrance to the course is now located and occasionally reach the green with their second shots."

That said, perennially hard, unwatered fairways meant that many drives ended up in the shadow of this tree. "When confronted by the big elm on 9, some of the skilled players would try to slice their wood shots around the tree," Nolan continues. "Sometimes the slice did not materialize, and the ball would go onto Dover Road and hit one of the houses with a loud bang. I guess the houses were better insulated back then, because no one ever popped out to determine what happened while we boldly walked across their lawns and poked into their shrubbery. Those truly were different times."

For all this change, once it was transformed into a par-5 in 1928, the hole's basic challenges have remained the same, and they are considerable. Dover Road closely

FACING PAGE: Wellesley alumna Kathy Hoang '98 tees off from the forward tee. She worked in the College investment office until the spring of 2003.

AT LEFT: Wellesley High School golf team member Liz McCabe lines up her putt in the fall of 2002 while teammates Clint Johnson, Dana Goheen, and Tony Rulli observe. Johnson and Goheen were the golf team's co-captains and, later on, Liz McCabe was on the golf team at Fairfield University in Connecticut.

Ann Cunningham and Bill Hudson

Bill Hudson grew up in Newton and caddied at Woodland GC. He moved to Wellesley in 1938 and started playing at Nehoiden in 1948. Plays with a cross-handed grip. Early on, a pro told him to leave well enough alone and his handicap has been as low as a 9. Ann Harby Cunningham grew up in Scarsdale, New York, and learned to play golf at Nehoiden from her late husband in 1960. When not playing at Nehoiden, Ann and Bill travel extensively. Bill remembers seeing Judge Dewing play golf at Nehoiden.

covers the left flank of 9 for all of its 531 yards—all of it out of bounds. "Safe" drives to the right have the potential for additional out of bounds in the 1st fairway, and many a second shot has been hindered by the row of evergreens that separates 1 and 9. Under these trees, the presence of Fuller Brook is impossible to ignore, for what might be a straightforward recovery shot from rough (left or right) is inevitably complicated by this water hazard, which cuts straight across the fairway some 330 yards from the back tee.

Even if the player drives into the fairway, Fuller Brook still presents a serious obstacle. From the back tee, a player must be able to hit two shots a combined 335 yards to clear it; from the forward tees, it's a combined 265. It's always satisfying to get beyond the brook in two or even three strokes, but it should be noted that a handful of Nehoiden golfers can actually reach the green in two.

Having successfully negotiated Fuller Brook, we are left with a handsome but intimidating view. Framed by bunkers right and left, the 9th green is pretty as a picture. Yet this is easily the most difficult putting surface on the golf course.

While most of the other greens at Nehoiden are relatively level, the 9th is pitched back to front at something approaching a 6 percent grade. To put that in perspective, "severe" greens at new golf courses today seldom exceed 2 or 3 percent because modern bentgrasses, which roll so swiftly, make anything steeper "unfair."

Nehoiden's 9th green was built in the late 1920s, when the best bentgrasses rolled at 6 or 7 on the Stimp meter; at this sort of speed, a six percent pitch wasn't unreasonable. Today, the 9th green has been seeded with a mixture of modern bentgrass and *Poa annua*, an aggressive, indigenous weed. This blend of grasses can "Stimp" anywhere from 8 to 11 which, combined with a six percent grade, explains why it is so difficult to hole out on 9, and why it's so important to stay below the pin.

At the same time, players of all skills and strengths are understandably fearful at the prospect of overshooting the 9th. Should an approach fail to hold this putting surface and bound over the green, the chip back is truly treacherous—especially from a rough-bound lie. It's difficult enough to keep balls from rolling off the green when putting from the back fringe, much less chipping onto to its perilously sloping surface from an awkward lie at the aqueduct's base.

Sheilah Ciraso of the College's maintenance services department had an unusual eagle here a few years ago when playing in a fall employee scramble tournament.

Her team decided to use her drive and second shot, and her third shot—a seven-iron punch from under some trees on the left—went into the cup.

Of course, par at the 9th is a fine achievement—a gratifying conclusion to any round or, because this is Nehoiden, an incentive to go around again. The 9th is ranked as the number one handicap hole on the course from the forward tees and is the number two handicap hole from the back tees.

The section of Fuller Brook that runs through Nehoiden was called Dewing's Brook in the 1600s and early 1700s. The Dewings owned 800 acres between the Charles River and Dover Road, and Andrew Dewing's house—the first home to be built in what is now Wellesley—was 100 rods (500 feet) south of the aqueduct. The Fullers received a land grant further east in 1642, and their section of the brook was called Fuller Brook; ultimately this is the name it retained and, like the Dewings, there were Fullers in Wellesley for more than 300 years. Andrew Dewing would surely have known both John Eliot and William Nehoiden because he was in charge of the Native Americans when they returned from their internment on Deer Island in 1676 (at the time there were only 200 Native Americans in Natick and very few colonists). Edmund Dewing, a direct descendant of Andrew, is remembered playing at Nehoiden by several members and as a well-respected public figure and jurist by former State Senate Minority Speaker David Locke.

Cliff Sibley

An engineer at Norton and Varian, he is now retired. Grew up nearby, caddied for his father at Nehoiden, and remembers Judge Dewing playing the course. **Best Shot:** Hit the pin on the 8th (pre-1964 when it was the 2nd).

Sheilah Ciraso

In the College maintenance services department since 1983, she has organized outings at Nehoiden. Women's Club Champion in 1996. **Favorite Hole:** The 9th—partly because "it's the most inspiring" and partly because she eagled it.

Edmund Dewing

1892–1981—A 10th generation descendant of Andrew Dewing who first owned the land that became Nehoiden. Was Norfolk County district attorney and a justice of the Massachusetts Supreme Court. **Avocation:** Golf at Nehoiden

Karl "Chip" Case

College economics professor. Co-author of *Principles of Economics*. Lives in the Grove Street home built by Edmund Dewing. **Wildest Shot:** Drive on the 9th hit Dover Road, bounced onto the fairway, and landed ten feet from the brook.

Golf at Wellesley College

Nehoiden Golf Course is used extensively by the College and is played by virtually all of its constituent groups—from the president, professors, librarians, and students to the groundskeepers, carpenters, electricians, and cooks.

Almost 300 College employees are members of Nehoiden, and a third of them are in the President's Club—open to anyone who has worked at the College for 25 years or more and for whom membership is free. The employees arrange tournaments in the spring and fall and have free golf clinics in the winter.

Golf is still a very popular sport with the students, and the classes fill up quickly. Golf instructor Anne Batchelder reports that each year from 100 to 120 students take the classes, largely as a function of the number of instructors available to give lessons. Students can take golf classes in the fall or spring, play on the team if they qualify, or just go out for a recreational round. They can use College-supplied clubs, bring guests for a fee of two dollars, and start their rounds the old-fashioned way by beginning on the 7th tee.

In 1893, the *Wellesley Magazine* reported that "Tennis, baseball, basketball, golf and scientific pedestrianism all have enthusiastic adherents." But when Lucile Eaton Hill arrived in 1882 as head of the gymnasium, the focus was on gymnastics and crew. Hill adjusted the focus when she introduced new sports, changing her title to director of physical training around this time. Dr. Channing, who advised the department and helped lay out the campus golf course in 1894, was very impressed with her, as was Mrs. Durant.

Before sports became a big part of the picture, each student had to take three hours of exercise a week in the gymnasium. And the physical examiner, Miss M. A. Wood, was there to scientifically measure their progress. Dr. Channing wrote that Wood "has already made a reputation for herself by the careful and accurate statistics she has made, founded on a large number of bodily measurements."

By 1896, gym requirements could be replaced by three hours a week of golf or another sport.

As recently as the 1960s, students were still filling their exercise requirements by playing golf—something that Wellesley President Diana Chapman Walsh '66 did one fateful day in her senior year (see page 98).

AT LEFT: *The golf team of the class of 1937*

FACING PAGE: *A golf class in an area close to the 7th tee at some time prior to 1925—the year in which a house was moved to the corner of Washington Street and Dover Road*

ABOVE: *A golf class in the 1930s or '40s on the hillside in front of the 5th green demonstrates a variety of backswings.*

FLAG AT CLUBHOUSE
INDICATES
CLASS IN SESSION
6 & 7
FAIRWAY CLOSED

Exercise programs are still required for a Wellesley education, and all students must participate to graduate ("there are no exceptions"). More than 40 activities are available, from classes in archery, squash, and yoga to team sports such as golf, basketball, and crew.

Wellesley's first director of physical training, "Gym" Hill, as she was affectionately known by the students, would be very pleased by all of this activity. She instituted Field Day and Tournament Day in the 1890s to demonstrate the various sports and drum up enthusiasm for them. Golf, basketball, and crew were always on the program, but so too were potato races and three-legged races. (There seems to have always been a degree of whimsy associated with College activities.)

The golf scores in these early tournaments tended to be on the astronomical side, although, to be fair, all beginners usually struggle a good deal at first. On Tournament Day in the fall of 1901, the scores ranged from 121 to 168 for an 18-hole contest. The winner had a low net score of 84 (her handicap was 37), and she received a trophy from Benjamin H. Sanborn, the first town member to serve as club president.

Hill was well organized and committed to going about athletics "scientifically." She formed the Wellesley Athletic Association in 1896 to give the clubs a strong foundation. Professionals were brought in to give golf instruction right from the beginning in 1893, and in 1897 *The American Athlete*, a magazine published in New York, reported on sports that were played at the College and stated that "Golf also has its club, whose number of members is unlimited. As it has the advantages of fine, expert instructors and plenty of room it becomes more popular every year."

But affection for golf was not universal at Wellesley. The apparently uninterested *College News* printed a letter on November 24, 1927, from a disgruntled student who protested that the paper's coverage of Field Day had excluded golf. The exasperated writer asked, "Must we have the captains of the senior and sophomore teams fight at Field Day with clubs in order to get a little attention?"

Until the 1960s, the College did not participate in intercollegiate sports for, as historian Alice Hackett wrote in 1949, "Wellesley's sports are organized to give recreation and healthful exercise." Field Day sports were played on an intramural basis by teams from either the classes or the dormitories.

It has only been since the fall of 2001 that the College has fielded a golf team for intercollegiate competition. Through the 2003 season, Kimberly Lapointe developed the first team, and Bill McInerney became the coach in 2004. He is from a golfing family: his father was on the pro tour in Europe and Asia, and his stepmother was a United States mid-amateur champion.

The team practices six days a week and plays from Nehoiden's white tees (courses used in intercollegiate play must be at least 5,800 yards). The golf team and others can practice in the warm and spacious confines of the Keohane Sports Center when the weather is bad, and golf classes are given there in the early spring. There is some irony in this, given that golf arrived on campus in 1893 due to an overcrowded gymnasium.

But much remains the same. Nehoiden member Cindy Peters '58 took golf classes when she was a student from instructor Eleanor Schroeder, who was something of a martinet and would yell out orders such as "Replace real estate!" if she saw a student taking a divot. Schroeder, a talented painter, often played with Peg Ball from the department of political science and Jean Glasscock, head of public information and editor of Wellesley's centennial history. Each of the women had trouble with a different hole and Schroeder did a painting of the three of them, exaggerating the difficulties of Fuller Brook (a roaring torrent) and the sand trap on the 5th (an endless desert). These women could readily have sympathized with some beleaguered Nehoiden golfers in the 1970s for whom this fearful sand trap became known as "Big Sahara."

ABOVE: *The 2004–2005 Wellesley golf team: Katherine Moyer '07, Jennifer Hazelton '07, Caroline Fischer '07, Elisabeth Wendl '07, Jennifer Jenq '08, Cecilia Yu '07, Susan Choi '06, Kirstin Neff '08, Victoria Lyo '05, Jennifer Stalley '08, Lauren Ino '08, Jena Roche '07, and coach Bill McInerney*

Photo by John Rich

Louise O'Neal
Director of physical education and athletics
Favorite Holes: 4 and 7 "the easy ones"
Comment: "Nehoiden is probably the only place where I personally experience the coming together of town and gown."

Bill McInerney
Golf instructor and head coach of the College golf team, he earned his college phys ed credits by teaching golf classes. He turned pro after his sophomore year, was on the mini-tour three years, and took *his* golf lessons from PGA pro Bob Toski.

Ann Batchelder
Professor of physical education and golf instructor
Favorite Hole: 2—"It's fun to meet its challenges."
Comment: "I like the way people can still play golf while classes are underway because of the configuration of the course."

Above: *When the orange flag is flying, the 6th and 7th holes are closed and either a golf class is in session (as it is here) or the College golf team is practicing.*

Sonia Berlin '04
She took golf classes and wants
to continue playing.
From: Katonah, New York
Major: Economics and Latin
Extracurricular: Photography Club,
Investment Society, Gardner Museum volunteer
Plans: Work on Wall Street, then get an MBA

Jee Eun Karin Nam '06
Born in Seoul, Korea
Home Town: Prague,
Czech Republic
Has taken golf classes and would
like to play more. She is interested in law
as a possible career.

Karen Goodenow '04
From: Toronto, Canada
Major: Economics and French
She was an aerobics instructor at the College;
took a golf class, then played in Arizona over
the winter break; liked the 6th hole but was
always concerned about hitting a passing car.

Jessica Desvarieux '06
Began learning golf indoors at the Keohane Center.
From: Armonk, New York
Major: English and history
Extracurricular: Editor of *Ethos Woman*, a
publication for black women, and program director
of WCTV, the College cable station
Plans: A career in journalism

The Wellesley Invitational Golf Tournament

In 2001, Wellesley held its first intercollegiate golf tournament at Nehoiden. Great care was taken to ensure that the course was in top shape; orange lines appeared on the course indicating where ground was under repair or where free drops could be had. The participants in 2001 included Mount Holyoke, Babson, Williams, Bowdoin and, of course, Wellesley. The event takes place, rain or shine, and has been attracting stronger interest with each year. In 2004, the Wellesley team won the spring and fall tournaments, thereby commemorating the 111th year of golf at the College.

AT TOP: The 2002 Wellesley Invitational banner adorned the Golf House.

ABOVE: The 2002 event was held on a rainy weekend.

AT LEFT: Two golfers on a misty afternoon

AT RIGHT: The scoring tent for the 2004 event

ABOVE: Wellesley won the Invitational in the fall of 2004. The winning Wellesley team is shown above with their coach, Bill McInerney, and included Jennifer Jenq '08, Victoria Lyo '05, Jennifer Hazelton '07, Susan Choi '06, and Katherine Moyer '07. Choi was the overall winner in both the spring and fall tournaments and had a score of 156 for her two rounds in the fall: an 80 and a 76.

ABOVE: *The Backwoodsman stood outside College Hall until it mysteriously disappeared in 1912. The base was found in the 1950s near the Waban Arches Bridge and ended up on Nehoiden's 9th hole.*

ABOVE RIGHT: *College Hall opened in 1875 and had rooms for over 350 students and faculty, an elevator, classrooms, a library, and a dining hall. Its construction was overseen on virtually a daily basis by the Durants. College Hall was destoryed in 1914 by a devastating fire.*

AT RIGHT: *Bill McInerney gives golf classes in the Keohane Sports Center. Ironically, golf was introduced at Wellesley in 1893 because the gym was overcrowded.*

No discussion of the College and its golf course would be complete without a mention of The Backwoodsman and his fate. This large marble statue was chiseled in 1844 by the American sculptor Henry Dexter. The artist died in 1876, and his daughter donated the statue—which had been on display at the Boston Athenaeum—to the College. And from 1886 to 1912, the Backwoodsman stared solemnly out across Lake Waban from the South Porch of College Hall.

Each May Day, for many years, it became a tradition for the students to give him a good scrubbing—so good that, in 1910, he lost his nose and a finger. However, in 1912, the statue mysteriously disappeared.

In 1914, College Hall was destroyed in a terrible fire and eventually The Backwoodsman was forgotten—until 1958, when dredging and rechanneling work at Fuller Brook unearthed its hulking marble pedestal near the Waban Arches Bridge. For some reason, it was placed on the fairway just before and to the right of the bridge on the 9th hole. At any rate, this is where Greenskeeper Tony Oteri found it when he came to Nehoiden in 1963. A short time later, citing safety concerns, he had it removed from play to the maintenance area.

In the spring of 2004, Nehoiden Manager Patrick Willoughby reported that the pedestal for the statue had been found at an off-campus storage site.

Why It Is that Golf and Other Sports Have Thrived at Wellesley College

Today, many colleges offer golf and many have 18-hole courses, although they tend to be relatively recent additions. Wellesley's golf club of 1893 may well have been the first college golf club in the country, and the College was among the first, if not the first, to actually have a golf course (see the Appendix).

The reasons for golf's early presence at Wellesley have virtually nothing to do with developing a facility for the game or acquiring one of the social graces. Golf was simply another form of exercise, and exercise was an important part of the founders' vision for educating women.

Henry Fowle Durant was a forward-looking man of passionate beliefs and would even lead the students on brisk walks through the campus to make sure they got their exercise. The fact that he and his wife decided to open a college for women was, in itself, revolutionary, since the general thinking in the late 19th century was that a woman's place was in the home. In a sermon he gave in 1877, Durant preached that "The higher

Lucile Hill organized the College bicycle club in the spring of 1893 and the golf club in the fall.

education of women is one of the great world battle cries for freedom, for right against might . . . I believe that God's hand is in it . . . that He is calling womanhood to come up higher . . . for noblest usefulness."

After the Durants' son died, one of their thoughts was to turn their estate into a school for boys. But their thinking evolved when they considered that there was a great need for women teachers. The nation was expanding west, and the loss of male teachers during the Civil War—coupled with the often poorly prepared women who replaced them—made the Durants feel, as Henry wrote in 1871, "there is no better way in which direct and continually productive good can be done in our own day than in helping to educate" women—to the benefit of all children.

To succeed in higher education, the Durants' believed that women should be physically up to the task. The centennial history of Wellesley—*Wellesley College, 1875–1975*—puts it this way: "In an era in which pallor, delicacy, susceptibility to fainting, tight lacing and a tiny waist were in fashion, Mr. Durant was a crusader. He put health as second among 'the five great essentials' in higher education and called upon students to be 'reformers and preachers in the new evangel of health.'"

If Wellesley was to spread the "new evangel of health" then Lucile Eaton Hill was to become its leading evangelist. She arrived at the College in 1882, a year after Henry Durant died, and became its first Director of Physical Training around 1891. She introduced a host of new outdoor sports including golf, developed the College's first outdoor playing field, and organized the Wellesley Athletic Association. In 1903 she wrote, "Cross-country tramping—not just taking a walk—for an hour or more, the body well set up, the heart and lungs working hard, is a glorious health giving exercise." Her thinking, which was already evident in the early 1890s, is right in line with the latest government pronouncements on exercise and health.

Henry Fowle Durant died in 1881 but would surely have endorsed Hill's ideas, including golf as an innovative way to get students to exercise. And he would doubtless be pleased by the absence of motorized golf carts at Nehoiden, where *everyone* walks and gets their exercise.

Henry Durant was an innovator and introduced tennis at the College on an English-style court that was the first of its kind in the region.

Director of Physical Training Hill transformed crew from singing expeditions on Lake Waban to tougher rowing exercises—rain or shine.

The Grounds

The shape of Nehoiden has changed gradually over the years, although not as a result of the large scale earth-moving and land-shaping techniques that have created many of New England's golf courses.

Aside from two major adjustments—the channeling of Fuller Brook in the 1950s and the gradual evolution of the entire area between the 3rd green and Dover Road—the land has remained relatively unchanged from the 1700s and early 1800s when it was farmland. Much of the land still shows the effects of the glaciers that retreated over 10,000 years ago, leaving the plateaus, hills, and steep drop-offs that are characteristic of glaciated topography in general and Nehoiden in particular.

A Landscaping Philosophy

The founders of Wellesley College believed with Frederick Law Olmsted that landscaping should accent what nature has provided rather than force and shape it along more formal lines. This viewpoint is based on concepts of independence and freedom coupled with a reverence for nature in contrast to the highly regulated and controlled approaches to both the landscape and society taken by, say, Louis XIV at Versailles.

As Wellesley professor and Nehoiden member Peter Fergusson points out in *The Landscape & Architecture of Wellesley College*, the grounds of the College were an important part of the Durants' vision of an ideal school for women: it should be situated in a park-like setting that would provide a restful atmosphere as well as a place for exercise, reflection, and communion with nature. Fergusson also notes that "For Durant, then, the notion of the park celebrated themes of liberty, freedom, health, mental well-being, and community."

It was the Durants' expectation that the students would become stronger and therefore more fit to pursue their studies and play a significant role in improving society. While Nehoiden may not be a dramatic illustration of the Durants' feelings about landscaping, it is part and parcel of their plan to provide a place of

FACING PAGE: *From certain angles, Fuller Brook appears to follow a carefully cut channel, which is exactly what it became in the 1950s when its course was contained and straightened.*

AT LEFT: *Nehoiden's fairways were originally cut with a horse-drawn reel mower similar to the one here. Ward Fearnside remembers the blacksmith's shop on Service Drive that made horseshoes.*

ABOVE: *Greenskeeper Alan Montanari on the triple mower is a full-time member of the grounds crew and stood in for Head Greenskeeper Eric Sinisalo when he was on leave during 2003.*

balls for more than 100 years, they also serve to instill a sense of calm reflection on the glories of nature, especially when one's ball has successfully carried past them.

Meadows filled with wild flowers were also a characteristic of the early Wellesley campus (at first referred to as a park), which explains why the 3rd, 4th, and 5th holes were called the "meadow holes" in 1900. In the early years there were no pine trees to separate the holes, and these three holes occupied what must have been a large open meadow—which is suggested by the photograph on page 45 of the golfer with the Waban Arches Bridge in the background.

natural beauty where exercise can be taken.

The Durants made a conscious effort to see to it that large and majestic trees were individually retained throughout the campus, and their early reverence for such trees continues to this day. While some may feel that Nehoiden's large trees are part of a scheme to make their golf game more difficult, or that they reflect an undue emphasis on conservation, they are part of the Durants' enduring legacy. And while the various large oaks, maples, and elms here have routinely deflected golf

Grounds Maintenance

Wellesley is said to have one of the most beautiful college campuses in the country, as anyone who has walked around Lake Waban or through the grounds of the College can readily appreciate. And it is no accident: the founders had a clear concept of what the underpinnings of their landscape design should be. Over the years, the College has worked hard to maintain the Durants' vision, and landscape architects of considerable renown have been involved with the grounds, including the firm founded by Frederick Law Olmsted.

The Hunnewells, an important force in the region's

Peter Fergusson
Professor of art history and art history dept. chair, he co-authored *The Landscape & Architecture of Wellesley College* and lives just behind the 9th green on Dover Road (collects enough golf balls in his yard to keep his game going). He has an MA and PhD from Harvard and is a Nehoiden enthusiast.

Patrick Willoughby
Associate director physical plant and Nehoiden manager, he has a degree in botany from Connecticut College. Was at Arnold Arboretum 17 years. Learned to play golf at Nehoiden. **Conclusion:** Golf is combination of trial and a lot of error and "You never know." (Has been on the 5th green in 8 and the 9th in 3.)

John Olmsted
Grounds superintendent
He attended Essex Agricultural and Technical Institute and came to the College in 2002 from the Arnold Arboretum where he was Head Arborist.
Favorite Hole: The 9th, because of "its topography and long approach"

Eric Sinisalo
Head greenskeeper
He was brought to Nehoiden in 1988 by then Manager Tony Oteri. He is a graduate of UMass Amherst and Stockbridge School of Agriculture.
Handicap: 18 **Best Shot:** A foot short of the cup on the 4th

horticulture, have also been closely involved with the College grounds, from the gift of Hunnewell Arboretum near the observatory to participation on the grounds committee. Interestingly, the Arnold Arboretum, which was designed by Olmsted and given considerable funding by his friends and clients, the Hunnewells, was the training ground for two key people at Nehoiden today: Patrick Willoughby and John Olmsted. Willoughby is Nehoiden's manager and the College's associate director of physical plant (he was at the Arboretum for 17 years), and Olmsted is the College's superintendent of grounds (he was at the Arboretum for 13 years and is a distant relative of Frederick Law Olmsted).

Wellesley has always made a point of having experienced, hands-on personnel who see to it that the grounds are cared for properly. As Harriet Creighton, botany professor emerita, pointed out in *Wellesley College, 1875–1975: A Century of Women* (edited by Nehoiden enthusiast Jean Glasscock), "The devotion of one whole group of people must also be acknowledged. A landscape architect can plan, a landscape gardener can plant, but only if the supervisor of grounds and the individual groundsmen care for the plantings will the original conception take form. Wellesley has been extraordinarily fortunate in the employees who have watched over the growth of its plants and shrubs and lawns." This sort of dedication is also present at Nehoiden where a handful of people see to it that the course is kept in good playing condition despite wide variations in the weather and the necessarily modest budget allocated to the course.

Nehoiden's maintenance staff consists of a head greenskeeper and two full-time greenskeepers, as well as a staff of part-time workers. This crew does everything from rake bunkers and repair storm damage to write up guest passes and assure a degree of orderliness on the course. Most of the Nehoiden staff, full- and part-time, are part of the College's maintenance department and some work on other projects at the College when the golf course is closed during the winter months.

A 1960s member handbook summarized the role of this staff well: "The course is operated by a very few employees under the direction of the Grounds-keeper; they have the triple duties of enforcing the rules, acting as starter, and maintaining the course. They do their work conscientiously and with concern for the interest of the members. They have the full authority to enforce the regulations and we bespeak your full and sympathetic cooperation with them."

As the course has evolved, the tasks have become more mechanized and complex. For instance, the sprinkler system, installed a few years ago, is monitored by a series of electronic timers. The increasingly sophisticated grounds equipment is purchased with an eye to broader uses elsewhere on the campus and to increased efficiency of the existing staff. According to Patrick Willoughby, a triple-deck mower was purchased to deal with the rough when it was demonstrated that the mower could pay for itself by doing a job in two days that previously had taken five days to complete.

Below: *In 2003, styrofoam coyotes were enlisted to scare off geese. From a distance, these coyotes look quite realistic but are less so up close. Their locations are changed from time to time.*

Greenskeeper John Ehrmanntraut

Organization

Nehoiden represents a tiny part of Wellesley's physical plant; it comes under Pat Willoughby's oversight and represents about five percent of his job. Nehoiden fits into the College's organizational structure as follows:

1. The greenskeepers (Alan Montanari and John Ehrmanntraut) and the part-time grounds crew report to head greenskeeper (Eric Sinisalo).
2. The head greenskeeper reports to the head of grounds.
3. The head of grounds reports to the superintendent of grounds (John Olmsted).
4. The superintendent of grounds reports to the associate director of physical plant (Pat Willoughby).
5. The associate director of physical plant reports to the director of physical plant (Adel Rida).
6. The director of physical plant reports to the vice president for administration and planning (Patricia Byrne).
7. The vice president for administration and planning reports to the president of the College (Diana Chapman Walsh).

This reporting is intermingled with ongoing department meetings and is buttressed by people such as former Men's Group president Jim Donahue, who is a special assistant to Pat Willoughby and works on a variety of administrative projects both at Nehoiden and elsewhere at the College. It was Donahue who worked with the Massachusetts Golf Association officials who, as the College golf team began to take shape, visited the course in 2001 to adjust its handicap and slope. He also oversaw the installation of the computerized handicapping system and the photo-ID cards.

Nehoiden's management office is located in the maintenance area where the waiting list, member mailings, and bookkeeping were all overseen until recently by nongolfer Helen Sullivan who retired in 2004 and admitted to having played golf once at Sandy Burr years ago and that once was quite enough.

The Hunnewells, Horticulture, and Wellesley College

Horatio Hollis Hunnewell made a fortune in railroads in the mid-1800s and accumulated a large estate where he built a white mansion he called Wellesley overlooking Lake Waban. The land, when combined with his wife's holdings, included several thousand acres and became what is now known, along with the estates of his children, as the Hunnewell Estates Historic District. The Hunnewells have always had a strong interest in horticulture, as their involvement with the Massachusetts Horticultural Society, the Arnold Arboretum, and Wellesley College attest. One of Horatio's sons, Walter Hunnewell, Sr. (who played golf at The Oaks in 1892) and then his grandson, Walter Hunnewell (left), sat on the College grounds committee for many years. In 1892, Horatio donated a large administration building to the Arnold Arboretum, and more recently the family contributed funds for the renovation of a carriage house at the headquarters of the Massachusetts Horticultural Society at Elm Bank. In 1901, Horatio endowed the first chair in botany at the College. His daughter Isabella, who was married to Robert Gould Shaw (their estate was later transferred to the College and became the Wellesley Centers for Women), contributed plantings and funds in 1923 for the Horatio Hollis Hunnewell Arboretum on the campus. Over the years, Hunnewells have been members of Nehoiden, but the family connection was of little use to Horatio's great-great-grandson David Livingston who "survived eight years on the waiting list." Though not a Hunnewell, former state representative John Locke lives in the original carriage house of The Oaks and often walks its old fairways. Locke's opinion of Nehoiden (he has played as a guest): "I love it!"

Golfing Grounds People

Just about everyone associated with the grounds at Nehoiden plays golf. Patrick Willoughby learned to play golf here because he felt that, if he were to manage the course effectively, he ought to know the game and have an understanding of the course from a golfer's perspective. Nehoiden Golf Club membership coordinator, Jim Donahue, is a past president of the Men's Group and 2003 Senior Men's Club Champion. Greenskeepers Eric Sinisalo, John Ehrmanntraut, and Alan Montanari are all golfers, as are part-time staffers Bernie Rothwell, Len Poitras, Vincent Montali, Bill McMahon, Dick Dorval, Joe Marenghi, and Jim Whetton (also a former Men's Group president).

The Landscaping of Wellesley College and Nehoiden

Frederick Law Olmsted is considered America's foremost landscape architect. Among his achievements are New York's Central Park and Boston's Emerald Necklace, whose undisputed jewels include the Fenway, Jamaica Pond, and Franklin Park. He was also responsible for the Arnold Arboretum, which has one of the most outstanding collections of specimen trees, shrubs, and vines in the world.

Olmsted's thoughts about landscaping were very much in line with the thinking of Ralph Waldo Emerson and the Transcendentalist movement of the mid-19th century. These philosophers combined a high reverence for nature with a fervent belief in freedom and independence.

Henry and Pauline Durant were well aware of Olmsted and his work as well as of Emerson and the Transcendentalists. When Henry Fowle Durant was a boy, his tutor, Sarah Ripley, was a close friend of Emerson. And the Durants were friendly with Louisa May Alcott, Henry Wadsworth Longfellow, Dr. Oliver Wendell Holmes, and others of the Boston intelligentsia—in fact, many of them visited the College in the early years lecturing, reading selections from their work, and talking with the students.

The Durants' ideas about Wellesley's landscape were in tune with the thinking of their time. Their intent was to create a natural setting that would enhance the educational experience of the students. Rather than plant formal gardens with annuals and regular flower beds, the Durants tried to preserve the natural setting and emphasize its features. Walks were laid out through the woods, buildings were placed in a way that complemented rather than overpowered their settings, and meadows and large trees were made prominent. The result was a campus that was more like a park. In fact, the campus was called a park in the early years.

The Durants were very successful with their landscape plan, for when the grounds were later altered by the addition of playing fields, walkways, and new buildings, the students, alumnae, and faculty began to lament the loss of the "wild beauty of the park." In 1894, the Playstead and the campus golf course (and the buildings that ultimately caused it to move across Washington Street) were all partly to blame. As Peter Fergusson points out in *The Landscape & Architecture of Wellesley College,* "In 1894, students, alumnae and faculty formed a 'Committee to Protect the Aesthetic Beauty of the College Grounds and Buildings.'"

In the early part of the 20th century, as it began to expand, the College again became focussed on its landscaping and ultimately hired the firm of Olmsted and Shurtleff in Brookline. In 1902, Frederick Law Olmsted, Jr., a partner in the firm and the son of Frederick Law Olmsted, stressed the importance of open spaces and building locations that would accentuate the natural setting.

The same strong attachment to the landscape that was felt in 1894 spurred a similar response in the 1950s and 1960s. Once again the alumnae played a role in getting things back on track when construction projects and the incursions of the automobile began to clutter the landscape.

In recent years, Wellesley has gone through a phase of expansion in the northwestern section of the campus close to Central Street and has added the Keohane Sports Center, athletic fields, a parking garage, a new student center, and administrative and maintenance buildings. The College continues to balance the landscaping principles that the Olmsteds and Durants embraced along with the Durants' dictum that the Wellesley student be required to improve her health and strength for the tasks that lie ahead.

The Durants created a setting that provided opportunities for exercise and for calm reflection—a setting that golf simultaneously became a part of *and* challenged. The 1898 College yearbook showed just how successful the Durants were when a student wrote, "What more delightful exercise could there be than to wander about, golf stick in hand, over our beautiful hills and meadows, on a breezy day in spring?" and, "With the unusual advantages afforded by our wide, wooded ground and our beautiful Waban, the Wellesley Athletic Association hopes, by wisely encouraging and guiding the present vigorous interest in outdoor sports, to aid in giving the Wellesley girl 'a sound mind in a sound body.'"

While the thoughts and feelings might be expressed differently today, the challenge remains the same as in 1894: to maintain the character of a beautiful campus while providing opportunities for healthful exercise.

Ralph Waldo Emerson

Frederick Law Olmsted

Frederick Law Olmsted, Jr.

Golfing Groups

The Women's Group

The Nehoiden Women's Golf Association (NWGA) is a women's group within the general membership of the Nehoiden Golf Club. It has been around for as long as anyone can remember, but no one knows quite when it was started. It seems to have always been set up formally with a chair (or co-chairs) and an advisory board made up of the secretary, treasurer, and various committee heads. In the absence of bylaws, its structure depends on a membership booklet put out each year that contains, in addition to the membership list, the schedules for Tuesday morning play, special days (the opening Miami, invitationals, member-member day, team matches, and the final field day), committee chairs and assignments, information on handicaps, championship guidelines, lists of previous champions and chairs, and rules and etiquette reminders.

The number of members has fluctuated—going from 65 members in 1962, down to 44 in 1972, and rising to 72 in 1983 and 74 in 2002. Membership fees (paid in addition to membership dues to Nehoiden Golf Club), on the other hand, have risen from $15 in 1972 to $30 in 2005.

The season for what is casually known as the Women's Group usually begins in May with a coffee held at the Golf House and ends with Field Day, traditionally held just before Labor Day. It usually consists of a Miami tournament followed by "lunch and frivolity" at a member's house.

With the aim of having a good time as well as playing golf, the Women's Group has always tended to be a friendly, low pressure organization. This is not to suggest that the Women's Group does not take golf seriously. In fact, one of its members, Laddie Homer, was a close friend of LPGA star Patty Berg and almost turned pro in the 1950s. In 1951, Laddie won the Grace Keyes Class A Championship held by the Women's Golf Association of Massachusetts. A number of the Women's Group members have played in state tournaments, including Lou Sink, Jo Coleman, Marian Gubellini, Dell Murphy, and Doris Gardner.

According to Doris Gardner, the Women's Group Tuesday games began as 18 holes, but in more recent

AT LEFT: *2002 winners Priscilla Bartzak, Gudrun Carr, Kim Fletcher, and Sue Poulton*

FACING PAGE: *The Golf House is being used here for the 2002 Field Day activities of the Women's Group. A number of groups make use of the Golf House for their events, including the College employees for their spring and fall outings.*

ABOVE: Past chairs of the Women's Group include, in front row, Jeanne Blackwood, Caroline Smith, Mary Ward, Sue Poulton, and Jane Murphy; and in back row, Adele Beggs, Priscilla Bartzak, and Joy Mitchell.

years they have become standardized at nine. For Tuesday play, members are encouraged simply to hook up with others as they begin arriving at the tee, which leads to a greater sense of camaraderie within the organization as a whole. Each Tuesday brings a new "game" including: low gross/low net; blind holes; red, white, and blue on the Tuesday nearest the Fourth of July; four clubs; and two mulligans.

As of 1964 there were no club championships as such, but there were Class B and C cups. Through 2003 the NWGA organized an 18-hole championship open to all women players of the Nehoiden Golf Club. The tournament consists of two rounds of medal play, followed by a final round of match play. Only members of the NWGA may enter nine-hole championships, with A, B, and C flights determined by the handicaps of the entrants. In addition to the official championships, there are interclub matches. Probably started in 1984 by Cis Toy, in recent years they have been successfully organized and shepherded by Joy Mitchell. They are played every other Thursday with four teams of four players each.

From time to time cups have been donated like the Gaylord Cup in 1963 for most improved player (in 1973 this cup became the club championship cup), the Barnett Cup for the Class A champion in 1969, and the Dell Murphy Cup for most improved player in 2001.

The association has also occasionally elected to honor one of its members for exceptional sportsmanship, longevity, and service to the group. Cis Toy and Dell Murphy were elected honorary lifetime members in 1995 and 2001 respectively; in 1994 a bench was presented to Doris Gardner on the occasion of her 80th birthday and placed on the forward tee of the 9th hole; and in 2002 the annual member-member day was dedicated to Doris for her continuing enthusiastic support of the NWGA.

The group often holds its events and parties at members' homes as well as at the Wellesley College Club, and often the lunches are accompanied by skits and singing. In this way the women of Nehoiden are being true to the spirit, found in early references to the club, that whatever else the club might stand for, "in the early days ladies' golf at Nehoiden was for fun."

Laddie Homer
A Wellesley resident and Nehoiden member in the 1960s, she was an excellent golfer and almost turned pro. She won the Grace Keyes Class A Championship of the Women's Golf Association of Massachusetts and was a close friend of LPGA touring pro Patty Berg.

Cindy Peters '58
1936–2003—A scratch golfer at an early age, she won the women's championship in Rochester, New York, for many years starting as a teenager (but had to return the martini pitcher prize). She was head of the Wellesley Athletic Association and worked at the Federal Reserve Bank in Boston.

Karen Donahue
Was taught golf by her father, and later took lessons. She was on the golf, soccer, softball, and basketball teams at Wellesley High School and earned an athletic scholarship to Assumption College. She is manager of new accounts at Commonwealth Financial Services.
Women's Open Champion: 2001 and 2003

Mary Linnehan '58
Major: Zoology. Never played golf in college but wishes she had because she loves it. Started playing in 2000. She organized Rally for a Cure, which is a day of golfing at Nehoiden to benefit the Susan Komen Breast Cancer Foundation. She is originally from Montreal.

Group Gatherings

Various groups gather at or near Nehoiden to celebrate tournaments, simply to be with one another, or to pick up a little pocket money—including the Men's Group, the Women's Group, College employee groups, and, less formally, groups of friends, co-workers, and relatives.

CO-WORKERS' GROUP: *A group from the Wellesley College library golfs just about every Thursday at 3 p.m. Shown here are Carolyn Hasgill, Dick Schofield, Alan Goodman, Suzanne Beatty, and Karen Jensen.*

MEN'S GROUP: *The festivities tend to be casual, but the competition is taken quite seriously.*

WOMEN'S GROUP: *The Golf House is often decorated for the Group's events.*

SINGING GROUP: *The Women's Group often has its luncheons, accompanied by entertainment, at the Wellesley College Club.*

CHAMPIONSHIP GROUP: *2002 Club Champion Tom Kelley, second place Chris Garvin, and third Jeff Crawshaw*

COLLEGE EMPLOYEE GROUP: *Employee tournaments, held twice a year, are organized by Jim Ralli and usually include prizes and a cookout at the Golf House. This group won in the spring of 2002 and consisted of Tony Oteri (retired associate director, physical plant), Jim Hickey (former head greenskeeper, now motor pool), Jim Ralli (recycling coordinator, motor pool), Kathy Lewis (administrative assistant, office of the dean of religious life), and Mike Culcasi (project manager, physical plant).*

GROUP SALES: *Wellesley professor Marshall Goldman and his wife, Merle, are Nehoiden neighbors and have a number of grandchildren who try their hand at golf ball and lemonade sales on the 9th tee when they are in town.*

The Men's Group

The Nehoiden Men's Group was founded in the 1940s after World War II. An early member of the group was Fred Nolan, who had served in the U. S. Navy and, prior to joining up in 1942, had played the course in the late 1930s. Fred recalls that he originated and ran the men's golf tournaments shortly after becoming a member. "Initially the fee was 25 cents per event. There was a box built into the bulletin board on the 1st tee (now the 7th) with a slot for depositing one's quarter. I had a key to the box and picked up the money each weekend," Fred remembers. The prizes were new Sweetspot golf balls, purchased at discount in Boston.

Today, the group's membership numbers around 100 golfers of all handicap levels, and the organization sponsors events throughout the season. Membership, now $75, includes all events, and members no longer need to slip a quarter in the box toward the prize kitty. The tournaments range from the April start with the Four-ball Tournament to the Iron Man Tournament in October. The latter event is only slightly less daunting than its name suggests as it requires that only a putter and an iron of the participant's choice be used for all shots.

The current organizational structure of the Men's Group was refined and established in 1991 by Travis Nutting, who served as president from 1990 to 1991. Travis was assisted by Terry Tuytschaevers who was vice president. Also lending support in drafting the current bylaws were three Nehoiden members: Len Poitras, Jim Donahue, and attorney Frank Connolly.

The current structure of the Men's Group consists of a president, vice president, secretary, and treasurer, all of whom serve two-year terms. Election of new officers occurs at the fall meeting which is usually held in November or December.

Each year, the golf season is ushered in by a meeting of the Men's Group to discuss the coming season. For a number of years, this meeting has been held at the Wellesley Community Center on Washington Street, and the catering has been provided—at a very reasonable price and to the satisfaction of all—by Peter's Pizza. In earlier years, the group met at the Italo-American Club on Oak Street.

Back in the 1940s, Fred Nolan not only ran the tournaments but secured the prizes, maintained handicaps, and kept the records. A number of years ago, the group instituted the position of handicap chairman, a post long held by Charlie Gubellini whose tenure was not without controversy, as he never shrank from assigning handicaps based on his knowledge of a player's game, despite the scorecards submitted. Charlie often took over the job of running the cookouts. He barbecued the steaks and cooked up savory dishes of peppers and onions to help the players celebrate their victories or soothe their bruised egos.

Over the years, members of the Men's Group have been involved in various capacities with the tournaments of the Massachusetts Golf Association. Tony

AT RIGHT: *The 2003 Club Champions included Senior Championship runner-up Jim Foley, Club Championship runner-up Eddie Carens, Senior Champion Jim Donahue, and Club Champion Jimmy Alden. Through 2003, the championships were run by the Men's and Women's Groups. Beginning in 2004 they were designated as Open Championships and run by the course management office. The Open Championships are open to all golfers at Nehoiden whether or not they are members of the Men's or Women's Groups.*

Vahey, a member for many years, has played in a number of MGA tournaments and in recent years has served as an MGA marshal ruling on such delicate matters as penalty strokes and questionable lies. Vahey recalls playing golf with former National Amateur Champion Ted Bishop at Oakley Country Club in Watertown a number of years ago. Bishop began his highly successful golfing career by shagging balls at The Oaks course on the Hunnewell estate in the 1930s.

ABOVE: *Senior tour pro Allen Doyle (center, cup in hand) visited Nehoiden as Richie Howard's guest, and the members came out to greet him. Crouching in front row are Travis Nutting, Joe Coady, Steve Chapman, and Arthur Grillo, and standing Chad Callahan, Doug Byington, Richie Howard, Lou Sardina, Allen Doyle, Billy Tobin, Harold Andrews, Jim Montague, greenskeeper John Ehrmanntraut, and Jeff Siegel.*

ABOVE: *Past presidents of the Men's Group include (front row) Jim Whetton, Travis Nutting, and Terry Tuytschaevers; and (back row) Jim Donahue, Don Crawshaw, Fred Nolan, Brian Jordan, and Doug Byington.*

Steve Burtt
Developer of single, multiple, and affordable housing, he is a Wellesley High School and Florida State tennis champion who grew up a block from the course. Serves on the Board of Directors of the Men's Group. **Handicap:** 13 **Best Rounds:** Shot 76 twice in Men's Knockout Tournament.

Joe Coady
A runner who switched to golf around 1984, he is a physical education instructor in the Cambridge grammar schools. Served in the army in Vietnam. **Handicap:** 4 (in the summer), 8 (when school is in session) Tends to be long and straight off the tee.

Dennis Greene
President of the Men's Group 2003–2005 An attorney in a Boston firm, he joined Nehoiden around 1983. **Senior Champion 2002:** Won in a playoff (was so tired by the last hole that he gave up trying and drove 50 yards further than usual which, he believes, demoralized his opponent).

Jim Montague
He is Director of Guidance at Boston Latin School, and his wife, Helen, is a house mother at Dana Hall. A regular in the early Saturday morning Men's Group, Jim has been a member since 1991. **Handicap:** 11 **Favorite Hole:** 2 (eagled it) **Least Favorite Hole:** 2

Other Uses

Nehoiden has often been used for purposes other than golf. During the First and Second World Wars, Victory Gardens were planted near the holes, and until the 1920s the maintenance area, then known as "the Pit," was used for hot dog and marshmallow roasts by the students.

Today, most golfers are blissfully unaware of the many pleasures that local inhabitants get from Nehoiden. There are the children who run through the sprinklers on summer evenings, and the young and old who go out onto the course to view the fireworks at the College. Some notice how much cooler it is out on Nehoiden when going for a walk on a hot summer evening.

And when the stars come out, Nehoiden is a wonderful spot from which to view meteor showers, comets, and other celestial events. Then there are those who come to watch birds when the golfers are gone. A good many birds do seem to co-exist peacefully enough with the golfers and call Nehoiden home during golf season—including the mallards that paddle on Fuller Brook, the hawks that perch in the large oaks and pines, and at least one stately blue heron that inhabits the marshy area beyond the 4th green and, from time to time, can be seen gliding across the fairways on its long graceful wings.

Evidence of course uses by others is more apparent in the fall when the Wellesley High School cross-country track team runs along the Aqueduct and across the course. The College also holds cross-country meets at Nehoiden.

The trails around the course and along the aqueduct offer pleasant surroundings, and the absence of automobile traffic provides strollers and hikers a pleasant walk unspoiled by golf.

From time to time, rock climbers scale the face of the Waban Arches Bridge behind the 3rd and 5th tees. The climbers occasionally shout to one another, and it is an eery sensation to hear their echoing yells while trying to address the ball.

While most Nehoiden golfers are aware of the presence of Ward Fearnside, few know who he is. And "golf balling" is not a term many know, but it does nicely describe—in his own words—Ward's lifelong pursuit of the little white ball. While most at Nehoiden pursue it with flailing clubs, Ward utilizes an exceptionally handy device made from a length of light weight lumber and a tuna-fish can when he goes golf balling. Ever since he found his first golf ball at Nehoiden in 1919, when he was six, Ward has been

AT LEFT: *Ward Fearnside began searching for golf balls at Nehoiden in 1919 when he was six.*

FACING PAGE: *Wellesley College hosts cross-country meets at Nehoiden. Shown here is a meet of the New England Women's and Men's Athletic Conference.*

ABOVE: *Golfers rarely get a view of the impressive south side of the Waban Arches Bridge shown above. The north side of this bridge is just behind Nehoiden's 3rd tee but is hidden by trees. Rock climbers practice climbing and rappelling on its facade while others walk, jog, and run across it.*

hooked just as effectively as the most ardent golfer. He's never actually played golf at Nehoiden or anywhere else for that matter but has preferred to roam its acreage looking for balls, which he donates to the Boston Youth Golf Program at the George Wright Golf Club.

As a boy and through high school, Fearnside developed a going business finding, reconditioning, and selling golf balls. It was often a hazardous pursuit, as the two groundskeepers at the time, curiously named Bill Hopp and Joe Foot, were constantly chasing him off the course. He later conceded that they were most likely concerned for his safety, but he solved this problem by rising at 5 a.m. He reconditioned the balls by first soaking them in lye and then coating them with lead paint, pouring the white paint into his hands, and rolling each ball back and forth until it looked new, then placing it on a drying rack. Lead paint was not then known to be hazardous, but his mother insisted that he never recondition golf balls if he had a cut on his hands.

Fearnside sold the balls for 35 cents apiece, which was a pretty good price in the 1920s and '30s, consid-

ering that a postage stamp cost two cents, and the most expensive Silver King golf ball cost one dollar when new. He also cut lawns and tried caddying at Wellesley Country Club but, on balance, found that the golf ball business was less arduous and more fun. Over these years, he managed to save $1,000, primarily from golf balling, and when he graduated from Bowdoin in 1934, he took a six-month trip to Europe on the proceeds. While in Nuremberg, he was caught up in a huge rally where he suddenly found himself staring at Adolf Hitler, who was only 40 yards away.

On his return, Fearnside enrolled in Harvard Law School. In those years, getting a law degree was considered a continuation of one's education, although he admits that he did not especially "rejoice in the law." He served in the Second World War and was stationed in Hawaii, North Africa, and finally Italy, where he landed four days after D-Day. On one occasion, when encamped on a mountaintop in North Africa, he met General Dwight D. Eisenhower and several other generals who were particularly interested in the site.

Although Ward Fearnside may be fairly consid-

AT RIGHT: *While dog walking is frowned upon in season, it is perfectly acceptable when the course isn't playable. Front row: Jesse, Hershey, Shadow, Copper, and Mulligan; back row: Connie Walkingshaw, Philippa Biggers, Susan Fulton, Debbie Krieg, and William and Jill Creevy*

ered Nehoiden's ball hawk emeritus, he is hardly alone in this pursuit. Nehoiden regular Cliff Sibley began hunting for balls at Nehoiden in 1935 when he was 12 years old. His father, Walcott, had been a topnotch golfer at Amherst, so Cliff's introduction to Nehoiden was more than just boyish curiosity. It was in his genes. Cliff, who would become an engineer, approached the business of finding balls scientifically. He observed that a good number ended up in Fuller Brook and that the weeds and the current often made it impossible for the golfer to retrieve a lost ball. After giving the matter some thought, the young Sibley set up a net, a golf-ball weir, across the brook just downstream from the bridge across the first fairway to catch the balls as they rolled along the stream bed. He would check his weir every day or so,

fish out the balls, and then sell them back to the members. With his earnings he was able to pay for his first-year's tuition at MIT. Asked about his second year, he replied "It was 1943. I was drafted, and Uncle Sam paid the rest."

Nehoiden's hills and open spaces have proved to be perfect for sledding and cross-country skiing. One of the most popular hills for sledding is the one that runs from the small shed by the driving range back down the 1st fairway. Cross-country skiers generally use the aqueduct, trails in the woods, and fairways that don't abut hills.

While dogs are restricted from the course during golf season, they are welcome during the off-season and a number of people use Nehoiden's open spaces for exercising their dogs.

AT TOP: *The 1st hole has one of the best sledding hills in Wellesley.*
ABOVE: *Wellesley resident Doris Eyges uses the course for cross-country skiing.*

Nehoiden Observed

Nehoiden has inspired a number of people to personal expressions of affection and creativity. Over the years, poems, songs, drawings, paintings, and reminiscences have resulted—and the contributors range from a retired technical illustrator to the president of the College.

The sampling presented herein consists of:

• Excerpts from *a poem and an article* that appeared at the turn of the last century in the *Legenda* (the Wellesley College student yearbook) and written by students who either played golf or had a pretty good idea of what was happening out on the links.

• *Cartoons* by Nehoiden member Bob Saunders showing how things might have been when the course opened for play in 1900. Bob made a pretty good guess when he had his 1900 golfer contemplate the maple on the 2nd hole: John Olmsted—Wellesley's superintendent of grounds and former head arborist at the Arnold Arboretum—estimates that most of the big trees on the course are about 100 years old judging by their crowns.

• Excerpts from the *diary* of Katharine Lee Bates, author of *America the Beautiful* and one of the College's most revered professors. The excerpts were given to us by Melinda Ponder '66 who happened to be in the College archives when this book was being researched and who played golf at Nehoiden when she was a student.

• *A reminiscence* of her early golfing career by College President Diana Chapman Walsh, whose relationship with Nehoiden nicely intertwines her love of the game with the love of her life.

• *Drawings* of each of Nehoiden's holes by former member Chet Brimblecom for whom Nehoiden, combined with his artistic talents, provided an island of sanity at a point in his life when things were not looking too rosy.

• The club's present *logo*, designed by member Frank McDonald in 1954.

• *Lyrics* set to popular tunes by Doris and Don Gardner that are still sung at gatherings of the Nehoiden Women's Group. Music always played a role in Doris and Don's relationship. While Don secured his spot in immortality by writing *All I Want for Christmas is My Two Front Teeth* in the 1940s, Doris has earned hers through her devotion to the Women's Group which placed a bench near the forward tee on the 9th hole in her honor.

• *A poem* by Tony Oteri's daughter, written when he retired from Wellesley College, that celebrates his life as a caring father and Nehoiden as a cheery home.

• And lastly, an excerpt from an *interview* with author John Updike who played his first rounds of golf at Nehoiden in the 1950s. In it, he reveals—though not in the section excerpted here—that ease of play at Myopia Hunt Club, one of the top golf clubs in the northeast (he is a member), is just about on par with Nehoiden.

FACING PAGE: This drawing of the 1st hole was done in 1970 by former member Chet Brimblecom. At that time there were no trees behind the green, and as golfers came up the hill they were treated to a view of Galen Stone Tower. This was Brimblecom's favorite view on the course.

These ads appeared in the Legenda *during the 1890s and, in the tradition of College publications ever since, helped underwrite publication costs.*

Golf at Wellesley College in 1898

Excerpted from the 1898 Legenda, *the Wellesley College yearbook*

The at times cryptic discussion of golf that follows was written when the campus course (built in 1894) began losing holes to construction projects for Houghton Chapel and Whitin Observatory.

"It has been found impossible to trace the evolution of golf, owing to the large number of missing links. There are nine missing from the Wellesley course, but judging from its rapid growth, we conclude it must be passing through what is known in geology as a 'critical period.' Last fall, golf received a 'boom' compared to which a Western boom pales into insignificance. Twenty new names were added to the Club. It is true that the membership has dwindled somewhat by this time, but probably absent ones have only wandered off after their lost balls, and we have hopes that they will get back by spring. The days are gone when the passing stranger stopped to shed a sympathetic tear over the teeing grounds, under the delusion that they were Indian graves, and when irreverent outsiders jeered at the gentle golfers. Now those who come to scoff remain to play,—as who would not, for what more delightful exercise could there be than to wander about, golf stick in hand, over our beautiful hills and meadows, on a breezy day in early spring?"

Baby's ABC Book (selected stanzas)

By an anonymous student in the 1900 *Legenda* who either played golf or had a friend who did

C is for the Caddy
    Who costs a lot of chink
And is, therefore, but rarely seen
    Upon a Wellesley link

D is for the Wicked Words, —
    It is an ancient joke, —
Which upon the golfing links
    'Tis said are often spoke

E is for the Egotist
    Who thinks his game the best
And makes you talk of it all day
    I own I'd like a rest

G is for nothing else but Golf
    A lazy person's game
To those who play at Basket Ball
    It seems a trifle tame

P is for the Putting Green
    A smooth green square of sward
A course of rolling would improve, —
    But that we can't afford

How It Might Have Been

Drawn by Bob Saunders

Bob Saunders

A member since the 1960s and a Nehoiden regular, Bob's interest in art took him into a career in advertising. Now that he is retired, he spends his time doing oil paintings, making sketches like the ones shown here, and traveling.
Favorite Hole: The 2nd

2nd hole tree was never a problem in 1900

Well dressed golfers in 1900

The course was not always in great shape

Some things never change

Katharine Lee Bates

From her diary, 1878–1911, in the Wellesley College archives

October 4, 1900 . . . went boldly out to the golf grounds. Played over four links.

October 8, 1900 More proof. No golf.

October 20, 1900 Went over the full course this afternoon.

October 21, 1900 Margaret Cowling out to play with Miss Seabury.

October 26, 1900 Had a golf lesson from Mr. Clarke this afternoon. Wish I could serve a ball like him.

November 2, 1900 Played golf before Council with Willie Buckley for caddie. Quite the best fun out.

November 6, 1900 Lived through classes only to play golf, but had to leave the field for an At Home.

November 7, 1900 Had a fine golf game and went into the gravel pit. That was gurly weird.*

According to Pine Manor professor Melinda M. Ponder '66, Bates knew Old English and Scottish. Gurly means ill-humored or evil in Old Scottish, and weird means fate or destiny. So "gurly weird" would surely be an appropriate description for the outcome of any number of golf shots. Ponder is an avid golfer who played Nehoiden when she was a student and is Katharine Lee Bates' biographer. Bates is shown here with her collie Hamlet.

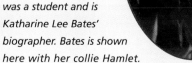

On Double-Deckers and Growing Up

By Diana Chapman Walsh, President of Wellesley College

In our Cape Cod house we have a poster that says "The sign of maturity is the ability to play golf as though it were a game."

My mother loved golf when I was a child. Golf and her many volunteer commitments were her equivalent of a career. She played on the club team at the Philadelphia Cricket Club and, because of her team matches, she was often late to pick us up at school. To mollify us, she would buy us ice-cream cones. It was always a double-decker if she had won. Making this contingent upon winning assured her a loyal fan club.

While raising my own daughter and struggling with the tension between career and motherhood, I often found consolation in recalling my own long waits in front of school, wondering when my mother would finally arrive to pick us up and whether there would be two scoops.

One of my mother's strategies to resolve her conflict between her passion for golf and her maternal duties was to take us out on the golf course from an early age. We were enrolled in the kids' clinics at the Cricket Club. Golf came naturally to me. I had a small bag with a 3-wood, 5- and 7-irons, and a putter. I learned to navigate the course quite skillfully with them. At age 11 and 12, I won the All-Philadelphia Junior-Junior Girls Championship, the beginning and end of my "mature" golf career.

From then on, I was always my own worst enemy on the course, expecting too much of myself and never being satisfied. All the fun went out of the sport, and I quit.

When I was a student at Wellesley in the '60s, I treated myself to a semester of golf to complete the physical education requirement, in which I had managed to fall behind. The election of golf resulted indirectly in my marriage and 31 years later the story enjoys wide circulation in the college community. It is one I used to illustrate, to those who inquired, just how my husband might deal with my becoming president of the college:

Like many of my fellow students, I met an appealing man at a Harvard University mixer and was pleased when he suggested we get together the next Saturday. Pleased, but hesitant. As I explained to him, I was duty bound to play a round of golf for my remedial credits. Chris interpreted this to mean that I was badly in need of instruction and offered to play the round with me.

After my triple-bogey 8 on the first hole he could not have been more supportive. After I proceeded to par or birdie every other hole on the course, he screamed "Sandbagger!" and ran back to Harvard to tell his friends he had met the woman he would marry. He loved the fact that I hadn't hesitated to beat him soundly.

When I was offered my present job, he quickly identified the best ancillary benefit, the location of the president's home—directly across the street from the college course. Although I rarely find the time to play, his passion for the game exceeds my mother's. He is a frequent visitor to our nine-hole Nehoiden Golf Club. As are several Wellesley faculty and staff—and many town residents who are members.

As I circulated through Wellesley in the weeks before my inauguration, feeling very much like Dustin Hoffman in "The Graduate" receiving advice from all corners—several people told me one of my top priorities should be doing something about Wellesley's sixth green which has a blind approach and borders on a busy street.

Ironically, when I attended a Harvard University symposium for new college presidents at the end of my first year in office, I found myself in the company of several female presidents who felt that women need the functional equivalent of golf to establish and nurture some of the relationships fostered in that fashion by our male counterparts.

Having played just four or five rounds since being back at Wellesley, my short game badly needed some work. Perhaps I was humoring myself to reflect that I was the only golfer among them. I look forward to growing up and returning to the game.

This article is reprinted in its entirety from the November 1996 issue of Golf Digest.

ABOVE: *The Durants purchased the Webber mansion as their home in 1864. It became the President's House in 1926 and is only 200 yards west of Nehoiden's 6th green. If Wayne Stiles' 1927 plan for an 18-hole layout had been effected, its 3rd green and 4th tee would have been right across the street. Another benefit for the house's residents would doubtless have been a regular supply of golf balls deposited in the front yard by Nehoiden golfers.*

Drawings of Nehoiden's Holes

By Warren "Chet" Brimblecom

Chet Brimblecom
A member with his wife during the 1960s, he is retired now and has lived on Cape Cod since 1985. He was a technical illustrator for several large engineering firms in Boston and New York.
Favorite Hole: The 5th

Chet Brimblecom's drawings of various views of the holes at Nehoiden hang in many members' homes and were made into note cards by the Women's Group that some members still use. When contacted, he sent us this reply:

"I did the drawings in late August and early September of 1970. I had just been laid off from a Boston engineering company where I had been a technical illustrator and then a technical writer. I was not in a happy frame of mind so went out and played Nehoiden 30 days in a row. I took a sketch pad with me and stood in the middle of the fairways and made my preliminary sketches. Refined them later at home. I actually did ten drawings (two of the first hole). I still have the ten originals and a few prints of six of them. In the spring of 1971, I went back to work with a different Boston engineering firm and stayed with them in Boston and New York until early retirement in 1985.

In 1970 there was no railing on the bridge of No. 1 (I assume there is by now). My wife and I went on the Nehoiden waiting list shortly after moving to Wellesley in 1952 and we think we made it to mem-

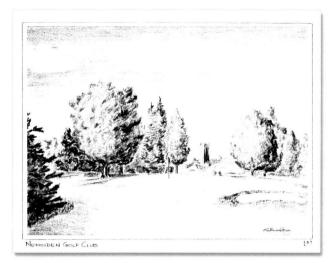

bership in the early to mid 60s. I think my favorite hole was the 5th because of the challenge of the big sand trap and the elevated green. My favorite drawing is of the 1st green because it shows the college tower. I'm sure that today everything is very different and not much looks the same. I haven't seen the course since 1975 when we left Wellesley. I play golf here in Yarmouth usually two to three times a week and it is still the best pastime there is."

Chet's drawings are an interesting record of how some things at Nehoiden have changed over the past 34 years. Railings have appeared on the bridge over Fuller Brook, a screen of trees now blocks the view of Galen Stone Tower on the 1st hole (and shots from going into the ravine behind the green), and a tree that was behind the 6th green has disappeared. The telephone poles on Washington Street seem smaller, and the goose neck street lamps have yet to make their helpful appearance.

Nehoiden's Logo

By Frank McDonald

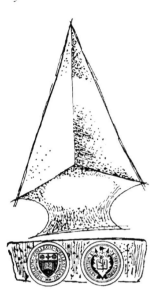

The club's emblem was redrawn by Nehoiden member Frank McDonald in 1954, and it features the seals of both the town and the College. He used to play in a foursome with John Anderson for many years on Saturday mornings.

When the Wellesley Golf Club was officially renamed Nehoiden in 1927, a new emblem also appeared—a simplified line drawing of an arrowhead (see pages 16 and 104). Judging from proofs in the archives, The Wellesley Press may have contributed the cards in exchange for having its name appear on the back panel. In a draft version of the scorecard, the Waban Steam Laundry that was on the corner of Cottage and Washington Streets has its name sketched in on the back of the proposed card.

Adaptations of Popular Songs

By Doris and Don Gardner

Doris Gardner has always been musical and has loved golf from an early age. So what better expression of her feelings about the game and the Women's Group and Nehoiden than her and Don's many lyrics—a few of which are reprinted here. Several were sung as recently as August 12, 2003, at the Women's Group luncheon at the Wellesley College Club.

Mulligan

(Sing to the tune of *Harrigan*)
M. U. double L. I .G. A. N. spells mulligan.
Every time I hit one off the very first tee, I get the feelin' they're all lookin' at me.
M. U. double L. I .G. A. N. for fun?
It's my game, and a shame
That I whiffed that ball off the tee.
Mulligan, just one?

What Is This Thing Called Golf?

(Sing to the tune of *What Is This Thing Called Love?*)
What is this thing called golf?
This funny game called golf
Why do I like this misery
And let it make a fool out of me?
I saw a course one wonderful day
And brought some clubs
'Cause I wanted to play
Now I ask you Doc
When my game is off
Who needs this game, called golf?

The Happy Golfer

(Sing to the tune of *The Happy Wanderer*)
I love to go a golfing now,
Along Nehoiden track.
And as I go I love to sing
My golf clubs on my back.
On the tee – you and me;
What a drive, see it fly
Ha, Ha, Ha – Ha, Ha, Ha
Oh, what fun, it's alive,
My golf clubs on my back.

I wave my hat to all I meet,
And they wave back to me.
And black birds call so loud and sweet,
From every green and tee.
On the tee, you and me,
Oh, what fun, to see it fly!
Ha, Ha, Ha—Ha, Ha, Ha
What a drive! A par 5!
My golf clubs on my back.

Bye Bye Golf Ball

(Sing to the tune of *Bye Bye Black Bird*)
Pack my clubs and my chapeau.
Here I go, swinging low.
Bye, bye, golf ball.
Everybody waits for me,
'Cause I sliced one off the tee.
Bye, bye golf ball.
No one here can love or even stand me,
I play all alone out on the prairie.
Take my cart, don't be polite
I'll arrive late tonight
Golf ball, bye, bye.

Bewitched, Bothered and Bewildered by Golf

(Sing to the tune of *Bewitched, Bothered and Bewildered*)
We're wild again—beguiled again
A whimpering, simpering child again,
Bewitched, bothered and bewildered, are we.
We hit that ball—and we miss that ball.
We shank, and we hook, and we overswing.
Bewitched, bothered and bewildered are we.
In the brook on the 1st tee,
In the pond on the 3rd,*
In the trap on the 5th,
Why do we play—this game yet?
Tomorrow comes,
We're on that tee.
Where else do you think
we would rather be?
Bewitched, bothered and bewildered—by golf!

*Until 1962, there was a marshy area given to flooding in front of the 3rd tee.

A Poem of Tribute to Tony Oteri

By Jennifer Oteri Sarrasin

When Tony Oteri retired, his daughter Jen was inspired to write a poem. The first five stanzas appear below and provide a pleasant perspective of Nehoiden.

Remember

Do you remember rolling hills and long stretches of fairway,
Cool fall mornings and spring days full of play?
Quiet cold winters, snowmen in December, boots, gloves, and hats . . .
Do you remember?

Do you remember the practice fairway and retrieving shag balls?
Do you remember playing in the leaves in the fall
And kids coming in for dinner when you would call?
Do you remember?

Do you remember station wagons, bikes and sleds?
Do you remember going to The Shed for Keds,
And at the end of each day, tucking us into our beds?
Do you remember?

Do you remember the bridges, the arches, the meadow, the brook,
The playroom, the yard, the kitchen so warm
And even golfers seeking shelter on the front porch in a storm?
Do you remember?

Do you remember the sounds of the day?
Sprinklers, lawn mowers, voices at play,
The sound of golf shoes on the driveway?
Do you remember?

Jen Oteri Sarrasin
The daughter of retired Nehoiden Manager and Associate Director, Physical Plant Tony Oteri, she grew up at 41 Service Drive next to the 2nd tee. She lives in Northboro and is the mother of three children but doesn't play golf.

John Updike
Author and golf addict, he first played golf at Nehoiden in the 1950s. Later in the interview that is excerpted at right he notes that at Myopia, one of the most exclusive clubs in New England, a tee time is rarely required (a characteristic it shares with Nehoiden).
Myopia was founded in 1894.

Novel Ideas

By Gary Larrabee, excerpted from the August-September 2003 issue of North Shore Golf.

John Updike, a longtime North Shore resident, is one of the world's most accomplished poets, short-story writers, essayists and novelists. He has won two Pulitzer Prizes, as well as the National Book Award, the American Book Award, the National Book Critics Circle Award and the National Arts Club Medal of Honor.

In recent years, he has become a prolific and much-sought-after writer on golf, which has played a prominent role in several of his most successful novels and essays. In 1996, *Golf Dreams,* his collection of golf essays, anecdotes and short stories was released to rave reviews.

Updike is just as likely to be found on one of his many favorite North Shore public courses as he is on Myopia Hunt Club, his home course.

North Shore Golf: What were your golfing roots?
John Updike: My roots were shallow; golf was beyond my family's social station, and I didn't touch a club until my first wife's Aunt Dorothy put one in my hand on her Wellesley lawn, at the side of the house. I took a piece out of her lawn, but she told me I had a lovely natural swing, and I was hooked. She and I used to play at Nehoiden, in Wellesley, and I began to play by myself at the public courses in and around Ipswich. Soon I acquired some Wednesday afternoon partners, and there was no looking back.

NSG: How difficult has the game been for you to learn?
JU: Pretty difficult; my best handicap at Myopia was a 17 and now it's a 24. I think my basic problem is that I can't believe, with the irons, that I must take turf for a crisp hit, and that the arms should descend with the wrist-cock intact. I tend to hit from the top, with the usual feeble, pushed, and fat results.

NSG: Are you a good student on the lesson tee?
JU: No. I get uptight and feel intruded upon. I'd rather work things out for myself, as in my other fields of endeavor.

Appendix

Nehoiden Scorecard, c. 1930

A number of interesting points can be gleaned from this early scorecard. The length of the 4th hole (today's 1st) is given as 490 yards, which means that the card was printed when the 1st tee was on top of the Sudbury Aqueduct (1928-1931)—this explains the extra yardage as today's hole plays 451 yards from the blue tee. The card also has a stymie gauge which is no longer necessary as players can now mark their balls on the green rather than be required to putt *over* their opponent's ball. Messages encouraging faster play and divot replacement appear on the front. There is a minor mystery on the 3rd hole (our 9th) where the length is given as 540 yards—either the measurement was off in 1930 or the tee went further back than it does today. The long-departed difficulties posed by the barn and corn crib on the 5th hole (our 2nd) are dealt with on the back panel.

LOCAL RULES
U. S. G. A. Rules Apply

Out of bounds; (indicated by white stakes).
1. From tee, tee again, play next stroke.
2. From any other place, drop at spot from which stroke was played and play next stroke.

A Ball May Be Lifted and Dropped

When it falls close to the water faucets near the greens. No penalty.

When it is driven under the corn crib, or in, under or around the barn from No. 5 tee. Penalty of one stroke.

When it strikes telegraph poles or wires. It should be dropped as near as possible to the spot from which the stroke was played. No penalty.

When it falls in the cedars on No. 5. No penalty.

When it falls in the cedars to left of No. 4. Penalty of one stroke.

All brooks and ditches (unless otherwise specified by signs) are water hazards. One penalty stroke.

COURTESY OF THE
WELLESLEY PRESS, INC.
WELLSLEY, MASS.

Nehoiden
Golf Club

WELLESLEY, MASS.

NEHOIDEN

Your consideration of the simple matters of courtesy in golf is necessary to complete the enjoyment of the game for you and your fellow club members

PLEASE REPLACE DIVOTS

Outside

	Yards	Mass Rating	Par	HDCP STROKES	W+ L— HO		Yards	Mass Rating	Par	HDCP STROKES	W+ L— HO
1	300	4	4	7		10	300	4	4	8	
2	155	3.2	3	15		11	155	3.2	3	16	
3	540	5.2	5	1		12	540	5.2	5	2	
4	490	5	5	3		13	490	5	5	4	
5	285	3.8	4	9		14	285	3.8	4	10	
6	150	3	3	17		15	150	3	3	18	
7	285	3.8	4	11		16	285	3.8	4	12	
8	270	4	4	13		17	270	4	4	14	
9	375	4	4	5		18	375	4	4	6	
Out	2850	36	36			In	2850	36	36		
						Out	2850	36	36		
PLAYER						T't'l	5700	72	72		
ATTESTED						HANDICAP					
DATE						NET					

REPLACE THE TURF   KEEP MOVING OR GIVE WAY

STYMIE GUAGE

Inside

FACING PAGE: *This aerial of the course was taken for the town by Chas. H. Sells, Inc., of Charlton, Massachusetts on April 17, 2004, shortly after the course opened for the season. The photo was taken from 2,400 feet and the time of the fly-over was made between 11:53 a.m. and 12:29 p.m.*

Newspapers and Other Sources

Newspapers, magazines, and various College publications were all used as resources for much of our historical information and include *The Boston Evening Transcript*, *The* (Boston) *Sunday Herald*, the *New York Herald*, the *Wellesley Magazine*, *The College News*, the *Legenda* (the Wellesley College yearbook), *The Wellesley Townsman*, *Our Town* (Wellesley), and *The American Athlete*.

Two newspaper articles in particular have proven to be invaluable for giving us an idea of what the early College golf courses were like, and they are fully transcribed here. *The Sunday Herald* of May 20, 1900 describes the early campus course, and *The Boston Evening Transcript* of July 25, 1900 describes the course we play today—albeit considerably enlarged and with three holes that would be virtually unrecognizable to the players of 1900.

Interestingly, there is a present-day Nehoiden connection to one of these newspapers: town member Eddie Carens' grandfather was a sports reporter for *The Boston Evening Transcript* during the 1920s and 1930s.

The Sunday Herald—Boston, May 20, 1900

FORTUNATE COLLEGE GIRLS

The Wellesley Golf Club Has a Very Picturesque Course.

The grounds of the Wellesley College Golf Club with their broad level stretches of campus, skirted by woodlands, smooth meadows, crossed by tiny brooks, and rolling upland fields, present unusual opportunities for the popular game and have the added charm of beauty of surroundings. The Wellesley club was first thoroughly organized in the fall of 1896, though the course, laid out through the kindness of Dr. Walter Channing of Brookline and Mr. Hunnewell of Wellesley, had been in use for some time before that date. Its officers are Miss Gordon Walker, president, and Miss Mary Vail, secretary and treasurer.

It is through the untiring efforts of Miss Walker, who held her office for two years (and is also a member of the recently formed Arlington Club) that the club is in its present flourishing condition. There are 156 members including students and instructors, and, like all organizations for outdoor sport at Wellesley the club is made a means to the end of the trained physical ability required of all Wellesley students. It stands almost alone among golf clubs in not requiring a large fee of its members. Fifty cents a year, in addition to the established athletic association fee of 50 cents is all that the Wellesley girl needs to spend to enjoy her golf. The club even provides clubs for its members although a majority of the girls, of course, own their own golf outfits. Members, however, are expected to go over the course at least three times a week, and

freshman may elect the sport to take the place of required gymnasium appointment during the spring term. Instruction is furnished by the regular coach, Miss Harriet Noyes Randall, assistant in the Wellesley gymnasium, and they are expected to observe regular hours for playing. L. C. Servos, the well known professional, has been employed by the club to give instruction to its members and private lessons can be had at the wish and expense of the player during any part of the season. The Wellesley girl, therefore, seems peculiarly fortunate in her opportunities for playing this healthful and pleasurable game.

The college course, unfortunately, is not so praiseworthy as the rules and regulations of the club. For some months the Wellesley Hills Golf Club of 85 members, and the Dana Hall students who are eager for links on which to play, have been agitating the question, of making use, by arrangement with the college club, of a large tract of land, the property of the college, lying on Blossom Street, across the Boston & Albany tracks from the college grounds proper, running nearly to the Worcester Turnpike. A course of 3,000 yards could easily be laid out here, and it is very probable that this plan may be carried out in the future.

At present the course on the college grounds, though not long, is in fairly good condition. The first and eighth holes are the best. For the first hole the teeing ground is at the head of the campus, halfway between College Hall and the

Shakespeare House. This makes possible a long drive across the beautiful smooth campus. The second hole starts in near the Houghton Chapel and has a brook hazard where many balls are lost. To the third hole is somewhat a long walk, and the third, fourth and fifth holes are played on the hill near the new Whitin Observatory. Hole No. 7 begins on a hill in front of the observatory, whence there is a long drive over good ground to the Fiske cottage. The eighth hole is 400 yards in extent (the longest on the links) and runs parallel with the main street to the north lodge; the last hole ends the course at a point near the chemistry building. The putting greens are in rather poor condition.

The club has recently given a brilliantly successful play, to raise money for improving the course, and the result is $150 toward the establishment of a new links, if it is deemed advisable.

The grounds, however, are sufficiently attractive to lure many out-of-town players as guests of the Wellesley maidens. On every pleasant spring afternoon they are crowded with golfers.

As the recent Wellesley "Legenda" put it "On any fine and sunny afternoon, the observer may see short-skirted maidens brandishing sticks with a menacing air or wildly rooting up turf in their enthusiasm, while others go poking furtively among the woods and boggy places, seeking for 'that old ball I lost.'"

The Boston Evening Transcript

Wednesday, JULY 25, 1900

GOLF CONSOLIDATION

Union of Wellesley College and Town Clubs

Admirable Golf Links Already Laid Out to Be Used by the New Organization—Clifton and Lexington Fall Schedules—An Event for Women Players—Notes from the Links

A union of the members of the Wellesley College Golf Club with the golf players of Wellesley village, also those in the Dana Hall School, has resulted recently in the formation of a new organization under the name of the Wellesley Golf Club. For two or three years past the college club grounds have been growing more and more inadequate as the course has several times been abridged, owing to the erection of new buildings—notably the Houghton Memorial Chapel and the Wilder [sic] observatory. The college club, moreover, has not been an organization by itself, but simply one of the branches of the general athletic association. Where to go and how to make the change has been a perplexing question, now happily settled.

This spring the college trustees petitioned duly by the golf club, granted the use of the tract of college property bordering upon Washington and Dover streets in Wellesley, and running back to the aqueduct—a generous amount of land, having most desirable features for golf links.

Next the academic council of the college gave permission to the college club to withdraw from the athletic association; then the final step was the forming of the new club, with college, village and Dana Hall golfers combined.

Under the constitution as adopted at the meeting for organization, the officers are a president, vice president, secretary and treasurer. These officers are members, ex officio, of the executive committee, which numbers nine in all. There is also an effective grounds committee of five members. Officers and committees have been chosen with a view to balance, as fairly as possible, the several interests involved.

Golf experts pronounce the course one of the best of the many in this vicinity. Aside from the advantageous points included, it is one of manifold natural attractions. In the main, the course is on high ground and the views roundabout are unparalleled in beauty. Lake Waban and the college grounds are in the background from the start, Pegan Hill looms up in the distance on the right, and off to the east lie miles and miles of wooded hill country, charming alike in spring and autumn coloring.

As most of the land had been ploughed over within two years, the soil was in good condition for work, rolling being the only heavy labor necessary to put the going greens into temporary good condition. The course as now laid out covers about twenty-one hundred yards, of amply sufficient variety, with nine holes to play. A few desirable points—such as a brook hazard, for instance—have been left for development in the future, when there shall be more funds at the disposal of the club.

The first teeing-ground is nearly opposite the lodge gate at the main entrance to the college grounds, on the high land which forms a corner at Washington and Dover streets, and the first hole is located well across the plateau, giving opportunity for a long drive, over tolerably even ground, up to the edge of a natural hazard, formed by a gully. The teeing-ground for the second hole lies sufficiently far back from this hazard to offer about an even chance for going over or falling in on the drive, while the second hole is placed on the top of rising ground, close to Dover street. Here, also, begins the next drive, down over the slope to the Fuller Brook, so-called. Near at hand to this third hole is the fourth teeing ground, and the drive ought to take one up the hill again, but in a more southerly direction, to the fourth hole. Then there is a short carry, and the next drive is down over a somewhat ragged hill and out onto the meadowland for the fifth hole. Hole number six is from one corner of the meadow to another—a good long distance. Number seven is from the corner of the meadow back near the triangle made by the start for the fourth hole, but at the foot of the ragged hill. The eighth hole is by far the hardest of the course. Starting from the low land of the meadow, if an air-line is followed, the course is up over the projecting corner of a sand-bank, which has been roughly excavated in times past, and where, if the ball misses its mark, it is wellnigh hopelessly lost. This is a short hole, and the putting-green is on the top of a neighboring rise, approached through more or less of undergrowth. The last teeing ground, for number nine, is on this same rising land, and the hole lies just back of the first teeing ground at the start.

Work has been carried on upon the new links for the past four or five weeks, and the results, from the time and labor expended, are very satisfactory. The fair green is in fairly good condition, the teeing grounds are all in order, and the putting greens, while not yet brought to the desirable point of excellence—indeed this would be impossible in so short a time—yet give promise of good future development. The course will be extended to add another four or five hundred yards as soon as practicable, and it is hoped that a clubhouse may be had at no very distant date.

It is possible for playing to be begun upon the new course at any time now. But as the majority of membership in the club is among the college students, the grounds will probably not be used extensively until after the opening of the college. Oct. 1 has been decided upon as the date for the beginning of the club year.

There was already a considerable golf equipment in the hands of the college club, with some funds, which, added to by the village and the Dana Hall contingents have made it possible to carry the work thus far. A liberal interest has been taken in the laying out of the grounds, the committees have worked faithfully, and much friendly assistance has been furnished. Several members of the Wellesley Hills Golf Club have expressed a desire to join this club, also, and their interest is cordially appreciated by the members of the organization. Mr. Benjamin H. Sanborn of Wellesley is president of the new club, Professor Katherine M. Edwards, of the college, vice president.

A unique feature of this Wellesley Golf Club is the combining in one large, elastic association of "town and gown." The common meeting ground of a golf course opens a happy prospect of enlarged opportunity for closer assimilation between two bodies, naturally separated, in the main, by differences of pursuit.

Harper's Official Golf Guide, 1899

In 1899, *Harper's Magazine* published its *Official Golf Guide* that included a listing of all the schools in the country with golf clubs. This publication is in the USGA archives where golf historian David Normoyle points out that much of the information relating to the early years of golf is frustratingly vague or non-existent. Suffice to say, Wellesley was in at the very beginning and, with a number of other schools, did not have a golf course at first.

If a school had a golf club, but not a golf course, where did the members play? At Wellesley, they hit balls on the Playstead. At Ohio State University, which was founded in 1870, the students used local courses until 1938 when the university finally built its own course, according to the school's head golf coach Jim Brown. Students whose parents were members of private clubs could have invited them to play their courses as was the case years ago at The Country Club when the Harvard golf team was invited to play the course. And, if students were as inventive in the 1890s as they are now, it is not hard to imagine that rudimentary golf courses could have been laid out on college playing fields or on open land—which would have been far more plentiful in the early 1890s than it is today. At the very least, they could have gone into the nearby fields to hit balls.

We can see that Wellesley's 1893 club is the earliest on the list at the right. What we don't know is if Ohio State, the University of Chicago, Boston University, the University of North Carolina, or Western Female College, all founded before 1891, had a club prior to 1893 as there are no dates given for these clubs. Western Female College wouldn't qualify as having the oldest college club in the country as the school no longer exists. And, while BU has a golf team today, it does not have a club—if it had a club prior to 1893 it might be the first but could not be the oldest. A historian familiar with the University of North Carolina has no information on a golf club at the school in the 1890s, but that does not mean that one didn't exist.

And then there is the nagging question: how many colleges and universities founded prior to 1893 were unintentionally left off the list by the *Harper's* researcher(s) in 1899?

Where no date is given after a school's name, it is assumed that the *Harper's* staffer in 1899 did not know the date of the formation of its golf club. The information in brackets was supplied by the USGA history department.

Of the 23 schools listed here, the ten that are colleges and universities appear in bold type.

Wellesley College Golf Club

Lawrenceville (NJ) School Golf Club

New York Military Academy Golf Club [Cornwall-on-Hudson, NY]

Mrs. Hazen's School Golf Club [Pelham Manor, NY – connected with Pelham CC]

College Hill Golf Club (Union College) – 1896 [Schenectady, NY]

West Point (NY) Golf Club – 1896

Watervliet Arsenal Golf Club – 1895 [West Troy, NY]

St. Paul's School Golf Club [Concord, NH]

Exeter (NH) Golf Club

University of North Carolina Golf Club – [Chapel Hill, NC]

University of Ohio Golf Club – [Columbus, OH]

Western Female College Golf Club – [Oxford, OH]

Penn Charter School Golf Club – [PA]

High School Golf Club – [PA]

Swarthmore (PA) Girls' Athletic Club – 1897

Jarvis Hall School Golf Club – [Montclair, CO]

Hotchkiss School Golf Club – 1897 – [Lakeville, CT]

Pomfret School Golf Club

Chicago (IL) University Golf Club

Amherst (MA) College Golf Club – 1896

Phillips Academy Golf Club – [Andover, MA]

Boston University Golf Club

Harvard and Radcliffe College Golf Clubs – 1896 [Watertown, MA]

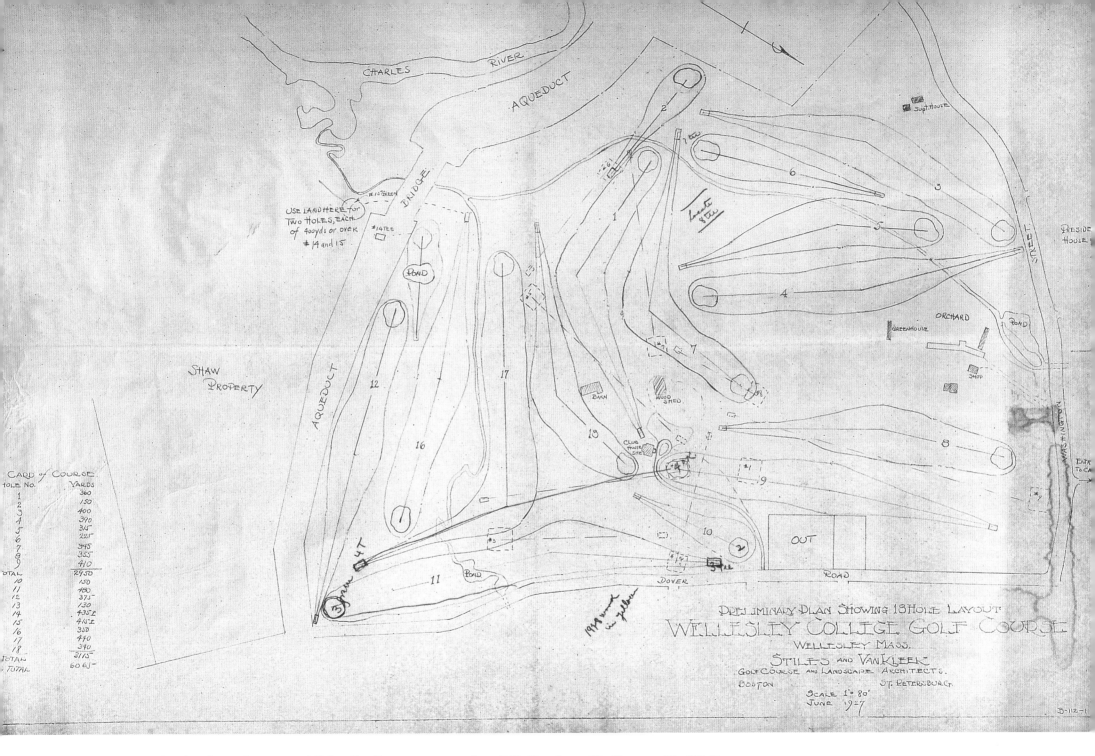

Wayne Stiles' Plan for an 18-hole Layout at the Wellesley College Golf Course

In 1927, golf course architect Wayne Stiles drew up the plan that appears above which, had it been acted upon, would have resulted in an 18-hole layout.

Bibliography

BOOKS BY WELLESLEY COLLEGE PROFESSORS & ALUMNAE

A number of the books that were used as resources for this history were written by Wellesley College alumnae or professors, several of whom have played golf at Nehoiden.

Eleanor Blair '17 witnessed the conflagration that destroyed College Hall in 1914. She was a teacher in a number of private schools including Dana Hall. Blair lived in Wellesley, became a photographer in her retirement, and took the photos that appear in her book. Her classmate, Eleanor Russell Reycroft, had the thrill of playing golf with Francis Ouimet.

Florence C. Converse was an editor of the *Wellesley Magazine* and graduated in 1892 just before golf arrived on the campus. A poet and playwright, she was an assistant editor at the *Atlantic Monthly* until she retired in 1930.

Peter Fergusson is chair of the College's art history department and Theodora L. and Stanley H. Feldber Professor of Art. A Nehoiden member, he lives next door to the 9th green.

Jean Glasscock was editor of *The College News* and graduated in 1933. She taught at the College, became its director of publicity, and was an avid Nehoiden golfer.

Alice Payne Hackett Harter, a 1921 graduate, went to the Columbia School of Journalism and wrote several books.

Lucille Eaton Hill introduced golf in 1893 and directed physical training from 1882 to 1909. Her first name is often spelled Lucile. It isn't known if she played golf.

Elizabeth Hinchliffe, a 1975 graduate, lives in Wellesley, and for several years was a speechwriter for the first President Bush.

James O'Gorman is the Grace Slack McNeil Professor of the History of American Art Emeritus at Wellesley.

John Rhodes is senior lecturer in art at the College.

Ola Elizabeth Winslow was professor of English emerita at the College where she taught from 1944 to 1950. She wrote a number of books and won the Pulitzer Prize in 1941 for her biography of Jonathan Edwards.

Blair, Eleanor. *Wellesley College and Community*. Wellesley, MA: Eleanor Blair, 1974

Bosworth, Raymond F. *I Am Nehoiden*. Needham, MA: Needham Historical Society, 1980

Bosworth, Raymond F. *William Nehoiden, A Man of the Massachusetts*. Needham, MA: Raymond Bosworth, 1982

Bradford, Gamaliel. *Early Days in Wellesley*. Wellesley, MA: The Wellesley National Bank, 1929

Cappers, Elmer Osgood. *Centennial History of The Country Club*. Brookline, MA: The Country Club, 1981

Clarke, George Kuhn. *The History of Needham, Massachusetts 1711–1911 Including West Needham Now the Town of Wellesley*. Cambridge, MA: The University Press, 1912

Converse, Florence. *The Story of Wellesley*. Boston: Little, Brown & Company, 1915

Converse, Florence. *Wellesley College, a Chronicle of the Years 1875–1938*, Wellesley, MA: The Hathaway Book Shop, 1935

Crawford, Michael J. *History of Natick Massachusetts 1650–1976*. Natick, MA: Natick Historical Commission, 1978

Crumbaker, Leslie. *The Baker Estate or Ridge Hill Farms of Needham*. Needham, MA: Town of Needham, 1975

Curtis, Frederic H., and John Heard. *The Country Club 1892–1932*. Brookline, MA: The Country Club, 1932

Dry, Dan. *Wellesley College*. Louisville: Harmony House, 1988

Fergusson, Peter, James F. O'Gorman, and John Rhodes. *Landscape & Architecture of Wellesley College*. Wellesley, MA: Wellesley College, 2000

Fiske, Joseph E. *History of the Town of Wellesley, Massachusetts*. Boston: Pilgrim Press, 1917

Freeman, Samuel, Esq. *Town Officer*. Boston: I. Thomas and E. T. Andrews, 1799

Frost, Mark. *The Greatest Game Ever Played*. New York: Hyperion, 2002

Glasscock, Jean, ed. *Wellesley College, 1875–1975: A Century of Women*. Wellesley, MA: Wellesley College, 1975

Hackett, Alice Payne. *Wellesley, Part of the American Story*. New York: E.P. Dutton & Co., 1949

Hayward, Allyson M. "Hunnewell Estates Historic District Cultural Landscape Report, Private Pleasures . . . Derived from Tradition." Independent Thesis Project for the Certificate in Landscape Design History, Radcliffe College, May 1997

Hill, Lucille Eaton, ed. *Athletics and Out-Door Sports for Women*. New York: Grosset & Dunlap, 1903

Hinchliffe, Elizabeth. *Five Pounds of Currency, Three Pounds of Corn*. Wellesley, MA: Town of Wellesley, 1981

Lysted, Virginia. *History of Natick*. Natick, MA: Virginia Lysted, circa 1975

Mahoney, Jack. *Golf History of New England*. Weston, MA: Jack Mahoney, 1995

Peper, George. *Golf in America, The First One Hundred Years*. New York: Harry N. Abrams, Inc., 1988

Schaller, Anne K., and Janice A. Prestcott. *Natick*. Dover NH: Arcadia Publishing, 1998

Servos, Launcelot Cressy. *Practical Instruction in Golf*. Boston, MA: Launcelot Cressy Servos, 1905

Shapiro, Mel, Warren Dohn, and Leonard Berger, *Golf, A Turn of the Century Treasury*. Secaucus, NJ, 1986

Sheehan, Laurence, ed. *A Commonwealth of Golfers 1903–2003*. Norton, MA: Massachusetts Golf Association, 2002

Slotkin, Richard, and James K. Folsom, eds. *So Dreadfull a Judgment, Puritan Responses to King Phillip's War*, Middletown, CT: Wesleyan University Press, 1978

Smithsonian Institution. *Handbook of North American Indians*. Vol. 15, *Northeast*, Bruce Trigger, ed. Washington, DC: Smithsonian Institution, 1978

Whittier, John Greenleaf. *Legends of New England*. Gainesville, FL: Scholars' Facsimiles & Reprints, 1965

Wind, Herbert Warren. *The Story of American Golf*. New York: Simon and Schuster, 1956

Winslow, Ola Elizabeth. *John Eliot, "Apostle to the Indians."* Boston: Houghton Mifflin Company, 1968

Women's Golf Association of Massachusetts. *On the Greens of Massachusetts: The Story of the Women's Golf Association of Massachusetts 1900–2000*. Women's Golf Association of Massachusetts, 2001

Index

Page numbers in italic type refer to a name or a subject in a photograph, caption, drawing, or map.

OVERLEAF: The 2nd tee in winter with the large maple devoid of leaves and the tracks of two walkers roaming the course